Other Books by William S. Butler and L. Douglas Keeney

This Is Guadalcanal

Day of Destiny

Fire in the Sky: America's Rocketry Program

Tragedy at Sea

No Easy Days: Drama of Naval Aviation

Secret Messages

CONCEALMENT, CODES, AND OTHER
TYPES OF INGENIOUS COMMUNICATION

WILLIAM S. BUTLER AND L. DOUGLAS KEENEY

SIMON & SCHUSTER

New York   London   Toronto   Sydney   Singapore

SIMON & SCHUSTER
Rockefeller Center
1230 Avenue of the Americas
New York, NY 10020

Designed by Anne Scatto / PIXEL PRESS

Butterfly and fort (p. 155) and Corporal Violet (p. 157)
© 2000 Laura Hartman Maestro

Manufactured in the United States of America

10   9   8   7   6   5   4   3   2   1

Library of Congress Cataloging-in-Publication Data

Butler, William S.
Secret messages : concealment, codes, and other types of ingenious
    communication/William S. Butler and L. Douglas Keeney.
        p.   cm.
Includes bibliographical references and index.
1. Cryptography.   2. Ciphers.   I. Keeney, L. Douglas.   II. Title.

Z103.B88 2001
652'.8—dc21   00-046368

ISBN 0-684-86998-5

ACKNOWLEDGMENTS

This book came about over cocktails at the Carlyle Hotel in New York City, a fine place for ideas. Our special thanks to Jane O'Boyle, who has been a constant source of encouragement over the last five years, and Janice Easton, our editor, whose delightful messages we will now miss.

Our thanks to Tom Hallion and Ed Farmer in Louisville, great tennis players and marvelous secret messagers; Tim Olson, a sheriff in Los Angeles; Jim Murphy, a fighter pilot in Atlanta; Walter McCord, cerveau non pareil; and Jeff Green, with the Bechtel Corporation at the DOE/Nevada offices in North Las Vegas, for their contributions to this book.

Thanks also go to The Los Angeles County Sheriff's Office, The Department of the Navy, The Department of the Air Force, and The National Archives.

LDK/WSB

CONTENTS

INTRODUCTION

This is a book about clever people finding ingenious ways to communicate. From card cheats to battlefield commanders to turncoat spies; from authors to engineers to weathermen in Washington, D.C.—they all had one thing in common. With unparalleled cunning, they used words, letters, colors, symbols, actions, phraseology, positions, objects— even smoke, light, and chiseled stone—to send or receive messages that they and their confederates alone understood.

When we embarked upon this book, we identified four categories of communication that fit our definition of secret messages. The first was grounded in the practical world—a study of the remarkable means and devices that people have used to move secret messages from point A to point B. Throughout time, one of the principal reasons for using secret messages at all was to bridge an otherwise daunting physical obstacle (a battle line, a span of distance, a noisy environment) while maintaining complete confidentiality in the process.

This we call secret messaging, the means employed to move a secret message between two people, or two entities, without being found out. The devices we catalogued ranged from an ordinary cloth belt on a Grecian foot soldier to the tiniest fragment of tissue paper sewn behind the label in a garment during World War II. Fascinating displays of ingenuity, all of them.

Our second area of study was individuals. Outside the formal code-making and code-breaking world of intelligence services, what means of secret communication have ordinary people devised to send secret messages? For instance, we studied the several cases where gagged and bound prisoners of war managed to successfully communicate with each other—and to the world—during their confinement in Vietnam. How did others come up with means of secretly communicating without any prior planning or without having any of the common tools of code-making and -breaking, much less the training? While we may never know whether Bill Clinton sent a secret message to Monica Lewinsky by wearing a particular tie, we do know that ties, chest ribbons, quilts, blinking, even the subtle shift of one's foot, have all been used to secretly communicate. In this endeavor, we found an enormous range of ingenious individual solutions to communication barriers.

Our third area of interest was accumulating and cataloguing actual, secret messages themselves. We knew of Victor Hugo's creative communication with his publisher, and we had previously written about many of the great D-Day communications sent to the French Resistance in the radio broadcasts of the BBC. Important milestones in this book and any other like it, no doubt, but surely, we postulated, there were many more. What words were used to tell President Roosevelt that the A-bomb had been dropped on Japan? We wanted to catalogue the instances where coded, imaginative real messages were used, in real life, and explain why. "Houston we have a problem": That was our aim.

Our final area of interest was the practice of messaging and coding as seen in our culture, today. We knew that more than one society, profession, community, or endeavor is accompanied, indeed, often enabled, by a set of codes. But what were they? Here we examined the means of secret messaging employed by homogeneous groups—hospital PA codes, police radio codes, construction crew hand signals, military hand signals, the commodities pits, auctions, baseball umpires, e-mail lingo, and other means of messaging used by a clearly definable set of people. 10-4? 10-4.

Two caveats. We decided early on not to include hand signals used by referees in football, basketball, and most professional sports, except that we uncovered some interesting, not-well-known nuances in baseball. Our feeling was that these signals, while sometimes falling into one of our four categories, were, by and large, overused in media accounts of sports and better left on the sidelines.

We also decided to be judicious and somewhat sparing in our use of World War II material. To say that secret messages from this global war would fill a book of its own is an understatement. Rather than tilt our material toward World War II, we sought to present lesser known and perhaps more interesting examples of secret messages at the expense of the bulk of material available on codes and ciphers. The transmission by our navy of a supposedly private message about our installation on Midway Island, for instance, while a classic story indeed, rests more squarely in the content of a book on ciphers and code-breaking. (The Japanese intercepted our communication and retransmitted it using their code for that island, "AF." We knew the Japanese intended to launch an attack against an island called AF, but we were uncertain which island that was. When the Japanese retransmitted our communication and substituted AF for Midway, we knew. Midway was the target.)

In the end, this is a book about imagination, about ingenuity and human creativity. From the earliest recorded history of man, indeed, through today and even into the future and across galaxies, people have applied, and continue to apply, their resourcefulness to secret communications. Author, publisher, dictator, philosopher, prisoner, card cheat, waitress, scientist, soldier, and many others have found ways to bridge a physical gulf with a secret message that, even if intercepted, would be gibberish to anyone other than the intended recipient.

SECRET MESSAGES

1:

SPECIAL DELIVERY

WE ARMCHAIR SPYMASTERS GENERALLY THINK of secret messages as dense, complex lines of random-looking letters and numbers that have no meaning until rearranged by an exotic code or letter-logic system. But not every good secret message must be rendered in code language. In fact, history is full of examples of secret messages sent in plain, uncoded text, right under the noses of the enemy. Successful messaging in these cases is made possible by ingenious delivery methods. In this way, secret messaging is sometimes akin to smuggling—transporting illicit goods past wary guards in a way that seems almost magical. It's human cleverness at its best, no less present in ancient times than it is today. Take the case of:

THE BALD MESSAGE

Centuries before the birth of Christ, Asia Minor was the scene of recurring military encroachments from east and west, and by necessity the birthplace of many clever methods of conveying a secret message (before speed of delivery held much importance).

In those days messages had to be delivered by human power, and secrecy was difficult to guarantee. When a messenger had to cross enemy lines, he would be thoroughly searched; a hiding place for a written letter would almost surely be found. A message disguised as a garment could be taken away. How, then, to overcome a vigorous search and get the man through enemy lines with the message intact?

Herodotus, the era's chronicler of events, tells us how. In *The Histories* he relates how Histaiaeus, governor of Miletus and plotter against the Persian ruler Darius, secretly communicated with a man named Aristagoras, whom he wished to enlist in his rebellion. It was simple, really. He shaved a trusted messenger's head, then tattooed the message on his bare scalp. After a few weeks of letting his hair grow back, he sent him on his way. After traversing Persian lines innocently, Histaiaeus's messenger is reported to have been brought before Aristagoras and said, "Master, shave my head." Which he obviously did, since the message set in motion a rebellion lasting almost six years.

Half the battle in secret delivery systems is not arousing suspicion in the vehicle itself. That's why common, everyday items like clothing make good hiding places, as can be seen in these stories:

Have a Belt on Me

The Spartan general Lysander and his troops were a long way from home. They had left Greece a month earlier on a military adventure that had been supported by their new allies, the Persians, who remained behind to safeguard Greece against their common enemies. A runner/messenger arrived at Lysander's camp one day. "I have a message for Lysander," he said, and was taken immediately to the general's tent. "What have you for me?" the general demanded. The runner replied, "I know not. I was told simply to find you." Lysander looked carefully at the man, and quickly saw a broad, leather belt around his waist. Branded into the belt, and running the entire circumference of it, were a series of random letters. Lysander knew what it was. Taking the man's belt, he wrapped it carefully in a descending spiral around a long wooden baton. As he wrapped, the letters aligned into sentences, until at last he could read them all. The message told him that Pharnabazus of Persia was double-crossing him and planned to seize Sparta for himself. Lysander returned and routed the traitorous army.

The Spartan baton was called a "scytale" and was one of the first known uses of military cryptology. The method simply required both the sending and receiving parties to have scytales of the same thickness. The sending party wrapped a leather belt around the scytale, much like wrapping the grip on a tennis racket, and either burned or cut his message into the leather. It was then unwrapped, rendering the message into a seemingly random line of letters, and worn normally as a belt. As such, it was innocuous and would not arouse suspicion. To read the message, the receiving party simply rewrapped the belt on his own scytale. If its diameter was the same as the sender's, the letters would align as the sender intended, and the message could be read vertically.

THE HAT TRICK

Professional spies still talk about the remarkable espionage abilities of a man who wasn't a spy at all—he was a newspaper reporter. Henri de Blowitz, in a long newspaper career starting in 1871, always seemed to be in the right place at the right time, with an inside track on monumental events. He invariably would be the first to break big stories in the *London Times*.

When the Congress of Berlin convened in 1878 to manage the aftermath of the Russo-Turkish war, everyone—including British Prime Minister Benjamin Disraeli and the Iron Chancellor, Otto von Bismarck—knew Mr. de Blowitz would be there, looking to turn the proceedings inside out for the benefit of his readers. Bismarck in particular had an interest in keeping the sessions quiet; his desire to remake the map of Europe would proceed nicely if public animosity was not brought against him. To this end he tasked his legendary spymaster, Wilhelm Stieber, with keeping de Blowitz out of the picture.

Stieber, with his army of street-level informants on high alert, and with the intelligence apparatuses of other nations also present, was confident that the formal deliberations were sealed shut from prying eyes and ears, and so informed his boss. It was incredibly confounding for him, then, to see de Blowitz's initial article in the *Times*, describing the entire agenda of the first day's deliberations!

Each day thereafter, with infuriating consistency, de Blowitz informed the world of the details of the closed-door discussions, and neither Stieber nor any other agent could figure out how he was doing it. Around-the-clock surveillance confirmed that de Blowitz had not been observed talking to anyone with any connection to the Congress; he received no mysterious packages or letters; he did not frequent any shadowy places or retrieve dead-drop messages. His behavior was utterly normal and innocent, and yet every day he had the scoop on who had said what, and would report it, sometimes word for word.

In the end, de Blowitz exceeded even his own high standards, publishing the entire formal agreement (the Treaty of Berlin) in the *Times* on June 22, 1878, almost before the ink was dry on the signatures and well before the formal release of the document to the press. His stature as the preeminent correspondent of the nineteenth century was assured.

It was only toward the end of his life that the secret of his success at the Congress of Berlin was revealed. The source for his articles was a confederate de Blowitz had managed to attach to the clerical staff of the Congress well before it even started. That explains how the information was so accurate and timely. But how did his inside man get the transcripts of the day's discussions to de Blowitz, since the two men never met, never talked, never even acknowledged each other's existence? It seemed that the two men dined in the same Berlin restaurant every night. On arrival each man would hang his hat—the same type and color hat, it turns out—on adjacent pegs. As he left the restaurant, de Blowitz would simply pluck the other man's hat from the rack and put it on his head. The secret messages were hidden in the hatband!

THE SHIRT OFF YOUR BACK

The German occupation of much of Europe in the early 1940s was accompanied by the violent repression and jailing of political opponents and the capture and imprisonment of civilians who sabotaged German operations in a variety of ways. These saboteurs, often members of paramilitary units collectively known as the Underground, were often interrogated and executed, but many thousands were thrown into filthy prisons where they tried to survive the cold, the malnourishment, and the disease. Almost worse was the fact that they were cut off from communicating with the outside world. Or so the Germans thought.

It has been the fate of many jailers, throughout history, to underestimate the resourcefulness and will of their captives. And so it was in the jails of Holland, France, Poland, and many other countries, where prisoners found a way to write long, detailed messages to their families, and to have them delivered without interception, and without benefit of coded language. How did they do it? When Red Cross workers were given nominal access to the prisoners, they brought clean clothing and toilet tissue. The tissue never went very far, but prisoners managed to save a tiny piece measuring about one inch square. This became a sheet of "stationery." With infinite patience and whatever writing implement could be devised (a sliver of wood or coal, a twig, even a fingernail), they would write letters using the smallest characters they could manage. Amazingly, letters hundreds of words in length were produced. When they were completed, they would be folded and placed in the small, looped clothing tag on the inside back of the shirts to be discarded. The Red Cross would gather them, remove them from the prison, and see that the messages were picked out of their hiding places and delivered. Even a careful rummaging through the clothes by diligent German guards did not turn up the messages, many of which survive today in museums throughout Europe, testament to human ingenuity and determination in the face of death.

2:

THE FALL OF TROY AND THE ERIE CANAL: WHAT'S THE CONNECTION?

Before the advent of radio, microwaves, telegraph lines, and cell phones, the extent of long-range communication from one person to another was exactly the distance one could shout. The megaphone was an audio breakthrough, though, amplifying the voice so that it could travel farther than before. Infantry officers of the eighteenth century used them to issue commands over the din of battle. Their effectiveness was still only in the hundreds of feet, though, and that's why bugles and other battle horns were invented. In the hands of a strong-lunged player, bugle commands could pierce the clamor and be heard perhaps 150 yards away, even farther on a quiet day.

Does that mean that messages or instructions in the ancient world could never travel farther than the length of a soccer field? Absolutely not. Even thousands of years ago sharp-witted men knew one important fact about the senses — that the eyes can see much farther than the ears can hear. They knew that the length of vision of a normal man standing at sea level is four miles. That is, standing on flat ground the most distant horizon is about four miles away. But if one climbs a hill and looks to the same horizon, the increase in the length of vision improves to thirty miles, forty miles, or more depending on the height of the hill and atmospheric conditions. Over the centuries many ingenious long-distance communications systems have been devised using that fact. Here are a few:

WHERE THERE'S SMOKE, THERE'S A MESSAGE

The dramatist Aeschylus tells us that the fall of Troy in 1084 B.C. was news so important that it had to be communicated to Queen Clytemnestra as fast as possible.

But she was in Argos, some five hundred miles away. Couriers could be dispatched: On foot, allowing for weather, uneven terrain, food intake, and occasional stops to rest or sleep, the courier would make it to Argos in about five days. On horseback, the trip would take a little over two days. But the Greeks managed, on this occasion, to let their queen know the good news by means of a telecommunications system only slightly slower than today's high-speed microwave transmissions. How did they do it?

In one of the first recorded uses of long-range communication at the speed of light, the Greeks arranged for fires to be lit at night on nine hills forty-five miles apart, with the hills chosen for their geographical alignment between Troy and Argos. As previously agreed, the queen would know that a visible fire meant a good outcome. As soon as the first signal fire was lit, the flames would rise fifty feet in the air. Since there was no ambient ground light at all at that time in history, the flames would be seen instantly by the fire team forty-five miles away on the second hill, who then lit their fire, which was seen by the fire team on the third hill, who lit their fire, and so on. In a matter of minutes the message traveled the length of Greece.

A TOWERING MESSAGE

The French army of the First Republic in the late eighteenth century developed a clever way to communicate messages at the speed of light over hundreds of miles. Under the direction of Claude Chappe, they erected hundreds of signaling stations on hilltops all over France, spaced three to six miles apart. Each station was equipped with a swiveling telescope and a wooden contraption that used moving, hinged arms and signal flags to send messages in semaphore fashion. The device was capable of nearly fifty semaphoric positions, enough to communicate the entire alphabet, plus a range of numbers and many special symbols. Signalers on station would scan the nearby hilltops with their telescopes for messages, and, having received one, would write down the message, spin 180 degrees, and pass it along to the next station in line as quickly as possible.

It was said that a message of roughly fifty letters could travel four hundred miles in an hour, passing through 120 signal towers!

TAKING THE LONG VIEW

The Indian tribes of the American Southwest used the elevation provided by the mountains that ring the area and the crystal clarity of light in that region to create an interesting line-of-sight messaging system that protected them from invaders for centuries. Standing at a moderate height and looking down at the flat, tan desert floor, one could easily see a man and his movements at a distance of five miles or more.

Knowing this, the indigenous tribes of the region developed a system of motion signals that enabled a solo scout on the desert floor to communicate what he was seeing to his buddies who were up on the mountain, out of harm's way. For example, riding a horse in a circle meant that something had been observed. If it was a herd of buffalo he saw, the scout would dismount and give the sign for buffalo—holding a blanket by the corners and lowering it to the ground. If it was a column of soldiers, the scout would ride back and forth in a zigzag pattern, indicating the motions of a cavalry engagement. This motion was generally used to communicate any kind of danger. If the scout bent to look at hoofprints on the ground, he could communicate the nature of the threat and the direction they were going by arm movements.

The tactical benefit of this method of messaging was the same for the Indians in the eighteenth and nineteenth centuries as it is for the digital infantry today—the main body of troops is held many miles away from the friction point while observers send real-time intelligence back to their commanders.

SMOKE SIGNALS

Speaking of Indians—a sturdy genre of movies and television in the 1950s was the cowboy drama. Usually made for kids, these "horse operas" were popular at the time, but are acknowledged today as being culturally biased against American Indians, wildly inaccurate about historical events, and childishly unconcerned with the real details of Indian life and customs.

A staple scene in these dramas was the "smoke signal" scene. Huddled in the rocks, pinned down by the Comanches or the Apaches, the cavalrymen would look up to see a column of smoke billowing in black puffs from a nearby hill. Ol' Sarge, the grizzled veteran of the Indian wars, would turn to his companions and translate: "They're sending for the rest of their braves to surround us. We're in big trouble now!"

But we wonder: Did the Indians of the Plains or the American Southwest really use smoke as a form of long-distance communication, or is this just another example of mythology or sketchy scholarship?

It turns out that some tribes did, indeed, use signal fires as a way to communicate over distance. And, amazingly, they developed this signaling method on their own, without any knowledge of the ancient European use of such signals, or any precedents in their own culture.

Thousands of years ago, hunters and fishermen of the tribes that inhabited the west coast of the United States used the high ground along the coast as signaling posts to communicate with their camps in the inland valleys. Signals consisted of beacon fires that could be seen for many miles when lit at night. There was no subtlety or any specificity possible with this method, but none was needed. The appearance of bright light in the western sky alerted the village to the fact that something big had happened—either there was a successful hunt, or a large haul of fish, or the presence of danger moving in their direction.

Indians of the Plains also used fires to signal over distance, but their method used the smoke of the fire rather than the fire itself. By covering and uncovering the smoke emitting from burning damp grasses, various tribes could send messages of moderate detail to their compatriots up to twenty miles away. The bright blue, cloudless skies of the Plains and Southwest provided a perfect backdrop for these signals, especially when the air was still. To begin a message, the fire was left burning for a while, to attract attention. Then blankets were held and released over the fire to create a prearranged pattern of smoke that would rise in the sky like a Morse Code message of dots and dashes. The patterns would be distinguishable by the number, length, and size of the plume. Again, versatility was not the hallmark of this message system, but it was malleable enough to communicate the basics— "Run for your life," "Prepare to defend yourself," or "Come here; we've got a bunch of soldiers pinned down in the rocks!" Best of all, the message was secret. The smoke code used was not well understood then, and is only slightly better understood today.

Boom TIME ON THE ERIE CANAL

Today we can communicate at the speed of light—186,000 miles per second. Tap the keyboard on your computer and, in a blink, a photon travels through fiberoptic cables spanning the globe, then returns to your computer just seconds later with the results of your Internet search. It is truly a mind-boggling affair.

In the early 1800s the speed of communication was a much different story. Still years before Alexander Graham Bell or Samuel F. B. Morse gave the world their inventions, the speed that a message would move was often limited to the speed a determined courier on a fast, and not easily tired, horse could move—about fifteen miles per hour, on a good path.

On October 26, 1825, fifteen miles per hour just wasn't good enough for a group of proud engineers and construction workers in upstate New York. They had special news to announce and they wanted it to travel at least at the speed of sound (1,130 feet per second).

Through clever planning and precise coordination, they got their wish, but if you hadn't known what was going on, you would have thought New York State were under attack. Boom! A cannon roared near the Battery on the Hudson River. A few seconds later, and a few miles upstream, a second boom answered the first. Then another at Governor's Island, then Fort Lafayette, and then another still at Fort Richmond—all the way to Buffalo, New York.

What had just happened? What were all those booming cannons about? In less than one hundred minutes, a message had traveled from New York City to Buffalo giving the marvelously good news that the Erie Canal had just opened!

3:

GOVERNMENT SECRETS

WHO OWNS the largest television network in the world? Who owns the most radio stations in the world? Who owns the largest film studio in the world? If you guessed AOL–Time Warner, you're wrong. The United States government is by far the most media-laden entity on the planet. Its productions in every form of media dwarf the efforts of Time Warner, Rupert Murdoch's News Corporation, and any other conglomerate you can name. Millions of pages of manuscript are published yearly by the Government Printing Office. Hundreds of thousands of pages of reports, newsletters, and bulletins come out of the individual federal agencies. Television networks and programming originate from the media offices of the Army, Air Force, Navy, Marines, Coast Guard, Bureau of Land Management, National Institute of Health, and countless others.

Indeed, federal power in the media is enough to inspire fear in every good conspiracy theorist in the land. Too strong a propaganda machine, they say, can become a tool for subjugation in the wrong hands. So far, though, the American public has resisted enslavement by the Department of Agriculture.

But the U.S. government does have its share of legitimate secrets to keep, and sometimes it is a good thing that it exercises a little caution in this area. In the stories that follow, you'll see why.

"PAUL DICTION SUNK JOHNSON IMBUE HERSAL"

In the late 1800s, America felt unbeatable. Giant factories, the product of the Industrial Revolution, sprawled across the face of new, growing cities; a new gizmo called the telephone offered instant communication; electricity powered homes and offices; and science was bubbling with confident projections that man would someday even control the weather.

Ah, the weather. Then, as now, the weather was the subject of endless morning conversations over a cup of hot coffee and spirited speculations about the message Mother Nature was sending with the color of an evening sunset. "Red sky at night, sailors delight," went the old maritime maxim. In truth, it was about as good as forecasting got at the turn of the century.

And that was a problem. Many people needed accurate forecasts — weather projections that were far more reliable than the old sayings and the timeworn nostrums. A farmer, for instance, had to know whether to do his spring planting today, or to hold off until tomorrow because a downpour was forecast. A fisherman would never lay his lines if he knew that a gale was somewhere over the horizon, nor would an ocean liner sail if there was a hurricane hovering offshore.

These were important concerns, indeed, and ones not easily met in an age that didn't have real-time satellite imagery, airplanes, or even sophisticated weather balloons.

But there were government weather stations. In the 1800s, these stations would observe the local weather conditions with anemometers and barometers and other devices, and send a daily telex to Washington, D.C., with their readings. Based on these readings, which were more commonly called observations, a national weather map was produced by the U.S. Army Signal Corps weather service.

There were problems, however, with the means of communication. Sending telexes was both time-consuming and costly, and the weather service was a penny-pinching outfit. Moreover, the weather service was a cautious service. It hated the public ridicule that invariably followed inaccurate forecasts, and more than once telegraph stationmasters had been known to leak the details of an observation, often at the expense of the Corps.

To minimize the expensive letter count, which was how telex charges were billed in those days, and to obfuscate the specifics of any individual observation, the weather service devised a special weather code that used a combination of abbreviations and short, specific codewords. "Paul diction sunk Johnson imbue hersal" is an actual coded weather observation. What does it say? "St. Paul, 29.26 inches barometric pressure, minus four degrees temperature, wind six miles per hour, maximum temperature ten degrees, dewpoint minus eighteen degrees. Observed at 8:00 P.M. and the local prediction is for fair weather."

Nonetheless, despite the pressure to cut costs and send these short, coded messages, it was often easier, and it was surely more convenient, to send messages uncoded, or, as it was called, "in the open." (When that happened, there were some commonsense safeguards. Certain words that might cause public panic were stricken—words such as "tornado" or "hurricane.")

Perhaps the most famous telex ever sent in the open by the weather service was an uncoded message sent to the manager of the Western Union station in Houston. Houston was close to another Texas city, a city that had a weather observation station, one that had been, for the last several days, inexplicably silent. This silence worried the weather forecasters in Washington, D.C. The telex sent to Houston forever marked the occasion (and the magnitude) of the worst mis-forecast in American weather history: "Do you hear anything about Galveston?" cabled Willis Moore, Chief of the U.S. Weather Bureau, on September 9, 1900.

Galveston, as students of history know, had that day been wiped off the map by the nation's worst hurricane, a hurricane that was never forecast, nor once picked up in the coded telex messages to and from the Texas city. People swarmed to the beaches to see the unusual waves; before the night was over, over six thousand of them were dead.

"WHY BUY A COW WHEN POWDERED MILK IS SO CHEAP?"

Nuclear weapons are the most classified topic in the world, and nuclear secrets are so guarded that revealing them publicly could be punishable by death. You would think that almost any official communication about these weapons—communications often sent thousands of miles by broadcast signals—would therefore be couched in impenetrable, organized, coded language. In fact, quite the opposite was true. Yes, encryption was commonly employed on formal message traffic, say from a nuclear test site to the laboratories in New Mexico, but just as often the secret language of nuclear weapons was nothing more than an impromptu hodgepodge of codes and personal whims.

Most people know the famous telex sent by then secretary of war Henry Stimson to President Franklin Roosevelt: "Big bomb dropped on Hiroshima 5 August at 7:15 PM Washington time. First reports indicate complete success which was even more pronounced than earlier test." But consider this message: "All gadgets were left intact." What could this message have to do with nuclear bombs? In 1958, a B-52 nuclear bomber collided in midair with a refueling tanker. Burning jet fuel, two mammoth military aircraft, and four hydrogen bombs rained down on a wooded area twenty miles from Hardinsburg, Kentucky.

As soon as the wreckage was found, an Explosive Ordnance Disposal team was on the scene, and the sentence above, "All gadgets were left intact," was one of their first messages out—a message that no doubt provided considerable relief to SAC. How do we know this? Because of the word "gadget." In the nuclear business, a codename was assigned to each series of nuclear tests and to each bomb in that test series. The first bomb fired at Bikini in 1946, for instance, was called the Able bomb, and it was fired during a series of tests codenamed Operation Crossroads. Redwood, Cedar, Dogwood, Poplar, Maple, Aspen, and Pine were some of the fifty-four codenames used during a test series called Operation Hardtack, and so on.

This system, however, got off to a choppy start. The very first test of an atomic bomb took place in Alamogordo, New Mexico, at what is now called the Trinity Site. Officially, there was no codename for this test, but through common usage it has come to be known as the "Trinity" test.

Similarly, there was no official name for the bomb that was exploded at Trinity, although the men at Los Alamos Nuclear Labs usually referred to it as "the gadget," or simply, Gadget. "Gadget," therefore, appears in the literature both as a formal name and as a general noun. Sometimes nuclear scientists and military users would say that "Gadget" was dropped; sometimes they would say that "the gadget" was dropped.

Absent any competing word, "gadget" thus worked its way into the nuclear lingo as the semiofficial codeword for the first nuclear bomb, and then for all nuclear bombs. The telex from the Kentucky crash site was calming because it quickly said that the nuclear bombs (the gadgets) had been found.

What about the words "Broken Arrow"? Today the phrase Broken Arrow has replaced the word "gadget," at least when there has been an accident involving a nuclear bomb. But despite the perception given by the John Travolta movie of the same name (featuring an Air Force jet that loses one of its bombs), Broken Arrow is not an Air Force term. Broken Arrow actually comes from Navy code. On July 15, 1978, the chief of naval operations put into effect the following nuclear codes for use in Navy message traffic:

- NUCFLASH: An incident involving a detonation or a possible detonation of a bomb that could create the risk of nuclear war between the U.S. and the U.S.S.R.

- BROKEN ARROW: Seizure, theft, loss, unauthorized possible detonation (but not one that might trigger war), non-nuclear explosion or burning of a bomb, contamination, or potential public hazard.

- BENT SPEAR: A significant incident other than an accident.

- **DULL SWORD:** An incident.

- **FADED GIANT:** A problem with a Navy nuclear reactor or the equipment around a nuclear reactor.

If all of that leaves you a bit cold and seems a little too analytical, an actual secret message sent from the Pacific Proving Grounds back to Los Alamos in 1952 might warm you up a bit. Six thousand miles and countless Soviet trawlers separated this distant test site at Eniwetok, where classified bombs were being exploded, from the nuclear labs back in New Mexico where the bomb had been developed. As preparations were under way for the explosion of a spectacular bomb codenamed Mike, the Los Alamos scientists nervously awaited word of whether their theoretical designs had worked. The bomb went off at 6:12 A.M. on October 31, 1952. The bomb blossomed into a ten-megaton fireball and forever changed nuclear design. How, though, were the results communicated to those scientists back home who were nervously biting their nails? The explosion of the world's first thermonuclear bomb was confirmed by using a secret message right out of everyday life: "It's a boy!"

Which leaves us with the message at the beginning of this section. The Mike bomb used a liquid fuel that required super-cooling and weighed eighty tons, which made it completely useless as a weapon. The second thermonuclear bomb was a test of a much lighter, but absolutely dry fuel called lithium deuteride. Would lithium deuteride work? At 6:45 A.M., on March 1, 1954, the firing charge was set off inside a bomb codenamed Bravo during a series of tests codenamed Operation Castle.

Did a dry fuel work? Read the message at the beginning of this section and you be the judge.

THE MONEY CODE

The American dollar may be the most stable and sought-after currency in the world, but for most of its life American currency has also been among the most easily counterfeited in the world. Back in the nineteenth century counterfeiters were so numerous that fully one-third of all notes in circulation were fake.

It's not that bad today, but even after the creation of the Federal Reserve Bank and its Federal Reserve Bank Notes (the money we use today) in 1913–14, the counterfeiting problem did not go away. Why? According to experts, the designs of the $1, $5, $10, $20, $50, and $100 bills have always been too easy to counterfeit. These bills, they say, lack the kind of artistic and design intricacy that discourages illicit printings. So beginning in 1996 with the $100 note, the United States began redesigning its currency, incorporating a wide range of new security features. The new notes have nine changes in them that the Treasury will acknowledge; the rumor is that there are other, undisclosed "secret messages" on and in the bill to catch counterfeiters. Whether this is true or not, the new features are sufficient to ward off the temptations of the new desktop printing technologies. Here are the changes found on the new $20 bill:

- Andrew Jackson's portrait is larger and the engraving is more detailed. Exact duplication of the fine engraving lines would now be very laborious for a counterfeiter. The portrait is off-center and therefore mostly out of the "folding area" of the bill. This reduces the wear and tear on the portrait.

- A fine-line wavy pattern has been printed behind the portrait and behind the White House art. Printed poorly, these lines create a noticeable stroboscopic effect.

- The Jackson portrait is printed in a near-invisible second location, as a watermark on the right side of the bill. It is visible when held up to a strong light. The number in the lower right corner on the front of the bill is printed in color-shifting ink. It appears green when seen straight on and black when viewed at an angle.

- The denomination numeral on the back righthand corner of the bill has been enlarged and set in a different font for the reading-impaired.

- The words "USA 20" are printed in micro size within the number on the lower lefthand corner of the note. Also, the words "The United States of America" are microprinted along the lower-edge ornamentation of the oval framing the portrait. Both these printings are so small that a magnifying glass is needed to read them.

- A polymer thread is embedded vertically in the paper to the far left of the portrait. On the thread the words "USA TWENTY" and a flag can be seen from both sides of the note when it is held up to strong light. The number "20" appears in the star field of the flag. This thread also glows green when exposed to ultraviolet light.

- A new Federal Reserve seal is printed on the left side of the note. Diagonally above it, a letter/number combination indicates the issuing Federal Reserve Bank. An additional letter has been added to the end of the serial number, which appears in two places on the note.

An interesting note: Look at President Lincoln on the front of a five-dollar bill. That's his face all right, but that's not his body. The engravers never got around to etching Lincoln's body because they already had a body engraving they thought would do just fine. So they simply put Lincoln's head on this man's shoulders. Who was it? Edwin McMasters Stanton, Lincoln's secretary of war.

4:

CODES IN CLOTH

WHILE HIGH-TECH TOOLS of the James Bond type inspire images of secret messages, it is the more mundane objects of the world that have more often been used to communicate secretly. A color, a shape, a certain knocking pattern on the door—these are the simple enablers of marvelously complex message systems.

What is a flag, for example, but a bit of colored cloth? Why, infinitely more. In the right hands, used at the right time and the right way, a flag can communicate a veritable encyclopedia of knowledge; send thousands of troops this way or that; surrender whole armies in a matter of seconds; wave off a near-disastrous carrier landing; inspire a nation to weep; or, in the case of Horatio Nelson, maneuver a mighty armada and save a nation from the grasp of a greedy Napoleon.

THE SIGNAL FLAGS OF HORATIO NELSON

Success in naval warfare in the early 1800s required that a fleet perform as a well-coordinated team. The fleets would be composed of different types of ships—small, fast, lightly armed frigates often called scouting frigates; brigantines; cutters; cruisers; standard-issue ships of the line, bearing sixty guns or more; and extraordinary flagships, larger and more profusely sailed and gunned than all the rest, on which the admiral of the fleet presided and from whence all tactical sailing orders for the fleet were issued.

In the event of battle with a fleet of similar size, there could be sixty or more ships turning and maneuvering around each other, which, to an outsider, might look like a blur of motion without coordination. In fact, these large engagements (at the start, at least) had a positional integrity and choreography to them made possible by the fact that the fleet commander could communicate with all his ships, even in the thick of the fire and smoke of battle.

How, in this era before radio or Morse communication, could an admiral deliver specific sailing and battle orders to one of his ships miles away? Conversely, how could the admiral get reports on enemy ship movements from his scouting frigates many miles to his front? The answer lies in the very inventive use of signal flags. The British were especially good at the use of flags whose graphic designs—lines, shapes, and colors—carried specific meanings. There were about thirty signal flags in all (about as many as could be reasonably carried and organized on deck), but, in fact, more than thirty messages could be communicated. How? Because each flag had a different meaning, depending on where it was hoisted above the ship. There were twenty separate signal halyards on a ship from which to hoist a flag. A certain flag on a main mast might mean "chase," but on a mizzen mast it might mean "retreat" or "close action." Flags raised at various positions on the ship could be orders to head in a certain direction or to a certain compass heading. In addition, flags were used in pairs or triplets, with meanings assigned to combinations of flags. Keeping it all straight was the responsibility of a "flag lieutenant" who took his signals orders directly from the fleet admiral. The system worked as well as could be expected, but its flaws seem apparent. Even with a telescope, the determination of exactly where a flag was flying on a distant ship was not easy to ascertain in normal conditions, and was often impossible in a pitching sea or in the midst of battle. Further, the billowing, dense smoke accumulating from cannon fire could rise above mast height, obscuring the flags completely.

Most objectionable of all, however, was the time it took to assemble and deliver a multiflag message. It could take hours to raise and lower many flags on many different hawsers to complete a message.

In the first decade of the 1800s the flag system was overhauled and streamlined, and just in time, too. A determined Napoleon was hoping to extend his empire to the British Isles and was amassing a fleet of French and Spanish ships to do so. It was only British naval power that could keep it from happening. One man in particular, the dashing Horatio Nelson, was equal to the task. At Trafalgar the battle was joined, and Nelson's use of the new signal system proved to be a decisive factor in the outcome.

But the most famous naval signal in history was sent not during the battle but before it. On the morning of the fight, Nelson asked his flag lieutenant, a Mr. Pasco, to make up this signal to the fleet: "Nelson confides that every man will do his duty." But then, thinking it was too egotistical, he changed it to, "England confides that every man will do his duty." He gave the signal order to Pasco, adding, "You must be quick, for I have one more to make, which is for 'close action.'" Pasco's memoirs tell the rest of the story. He writes: "I replied, 'If Your Lordship will permit me to substitute the word 'expects' for 'confides,' the signal will soon be completed, because the word 'expects' is in the vocabulary and 'confides' must be spelt," meaning he could signal the word with three flags on one halyard instead of seven flags raised and lowered one time each. Nelson acquiesced, and the signal "England expects that every man will do his duty" was hoisted.

Today the sentence still lives, committed to memory by all schoolchildren and burnished into the fabric of British history.

Revolutionary Hanky-Panky

New York in 1778 was a Tory kind of town. British army and naval officers mingled with their American sympathizers routinely and openly. To tap into this potential wealth of military intelligence, General George Washington and his spy chief, Benjamin Tallmadge, established a network of operatives that could gather information from the city and transfer it by circuitous routes to Tallmadge's headquarters in Connecticut. This network was called the Culper Ring, so named for the noms de guerre of two of the network's major players—Robert Townsend (Samuel Culper, Sr.) and Abraham Woodhull (Samuel Culper, Jr.).

The system worked like this: Townsend, risking detection from spy-savvy Brits, culled bits of intelligence from the neighborhoods around British headquarters, using both his social position and a general store as cover. He would encode a written message to Tallmadge using a combination of letter and number substitution codes. (Although no copies of the code book survive today, we know that the numeral 711 stood for "Gen. Washington"; 727 meant "New York"; 592 meant "ships"; 286 meant "ink"; and so on. The sentence "Dqpeu Beyocpu agreeable to 28 met 723 not far from 727" meant "Jonas Hawkins agreeable to appointment to meet Robert Townsend not far from New York.")

Courier Austin Roe then would smuggle the document to Woodhull at his home on the north shore of Long Island, where it would stay until Caleb Brewster, another link in the chain, sailed under cover of darkness across the Long Island Sound to pick it up. Brewster ran a considerable risk: British ships interdicted all vessels on the sound from time to time. Capture with coded documents would mean certain death.

For his own security Roe would arrive at different times and at different coves on each trip. This link between Roe and Woodhull was the diciest part of the operation, and the most subject to British scrutiny. The colonials solved this problem with Yankee ingenuity. Woodhull, not knowing exactly when Roe would arrive or where he would be, kept his telescope trained on the home of his neighbor, Anna Strong, whose views of the sound were better than his own. Strong communicated secret messages to Woodhull by means of her clothesline. When Brewster's boat arrived and anchored, Strong would hang a black petticoat on the line; a series of black handkerchiefs would then indicate the cove in which Brewster was hiding. For five years this simple system worked beautifully. This conduit of information proved invaluable to Washington, and the Culper Ring, despite aggressive British tactics to discover and disband it, stayed in secret service until 1783.

Eighty years later, at a time in American history when the nation was again in jeopardy, fabric messages played an important role in the flight of fugitive slaves to the north. Again, seemingly simple household items were used to complex effect in an ingenious messaging system.

THE QUILT CODE SYSTEM

The escape route to Canada and points north for runaway slaves in the pre–Civil War South was called the Underground Railroad. There actually was no road, nor road maps, nor any overt system of signs by which fleeing slaves could navigate their way. But the Railroad operated in a systematic way, through the dedication and planning of a network of people whose homes, churches, and businesses were way stations for small groups of slaves heading north. Thanks to recent scholarship by Jacqueline Tobin, we now know that there was a helpful system of secret directions and signals used by the runaway slaves to find the correct routes north, and to warn of the presence of danger.

As in all clever code practice, the directions were hidden in plain sight, in this case in the form of quilts. Under the very noses of their owners, slaves would sew quilts of specific patterns and drape these seemingly innocent quilts on the doors of their cabins or hang them in windows for the running slaves to see. According to Tobin, there were dozens of quilt designs, each one conveying a different instruction or warning, and each one conveying a proverb.

No one but the slaves themselves knew the meanings of the quilts, and their insularity as a group assured that no outsiders, and certainly no slave owners, would ever discover the real messages hidden in the fabric.

1. "Bear's Paw" ("Follow bear tracks to navigate mountain routes")
2. "The Drunkard's Path" ("Avoid capture by never traveling in straight lines")
3. "Flying Geese" ("Follow birds north, and to water when needed")
4. "Crossroads" ("Head to Cleveland, Ohio, where the escape routes meet")

HOBO MESSAGES

A nearly identical scenario played out in the 1930s, when another persecuted group wandered through America, seeking signs to guide them. This time it was hoboes who looked for the secret signs that only they understood.

The Depression and its economic hardships made tramps out of a lot of men. After losing their jobs they became wanderers, hopping freight trains from one place to another, working odd jobs or just asking for a handout. They often plied the same territory, and over time they "marked" towns, cities, and individual houses. If a hobo saw a certain symbol scratched on a wall or sidewalk in coal, he knew all there was to know about the town he was in and its people. How did he know? Because hoboes developed a secret language of symbols that served as indications to other hoboes of the town's friendliness or hostility. A sampling of their message system includes:

A nice lady lives here   They'll feed you for work   They've a dog—beware

Owner of the house   Get out of town ASAP   Police are watching
is at home

You can sleep in the barn   Good road to be on

5:

WEARING IT OUT

BEHAVIORAL SCIENTISTS would say that your appearance is not a random act, but a reflection of who you think you are. Your clothes, they say, send unconscious secret messages about you all day long. Maybe so. But some people wear certain clothes for an explicit reason—they really are sending messages.

Clothes can be an excellent signal, or an identifier, or a secret membership card. Or they can be an organizer. Case in point—on an aircraft carrier deck. A supersonic jet fighter is a lot like a finely tuned Formula One racecar—fast and agile, but easy to break. No wonder that pilots don't like just anyone touching their jet. In fact, the whole atmosphere of a busy flight deck makes them nervous. But the Navy has imposed order on the scene, and they've done it with clothes.

ON THE CARRIER DECK

If you didn't know better, you'd think that the activity on a carrier deck was pure chaos—a swirling blend of men, airplanes, and machinery. There is a lot going on, all right, but it is more organized than you think. The choreography of specialists doing their individual jobs on deck has been perfected over seventy years of naval air experience, and everybody knows what the other guy is doing. The colored jerseys that all of the men and women wear—purple, blue, green, yellow, brown, and white—are worn for a purpose, serving as job identifiers. Your plane needs gas in a hurry? Look for a purple shirt. Need to move a plane off the deck? Grab one of the guys in blue. A carrier deck is one place where you don't want someone's job to be a secret. Your shirt color tells the world who you are and what you do.

- **PURPLE SHIRTS**: Aviation fuel handlers, known collectively by the nickname "Grapes."

- **BLUE SHIRTS**: Airplane handlers, elevator operators, tractor drivers.

- **GREEN SHIRTS**: Catapult and arresting gear crews, maintenance personnel, quality control personnel, cargo handlers, hook runners, equipment troubleshooters.

- **YELLOW SHIRTS**: Aircraft handling officers, catapult and arresting gear officers, plane directors.

- **BROWN SHIRTS**: Air wing plane captains, air wing line leading petty officers.

- **WHITE SHIRTS**: Squadron plane inspectors, air transfer officers (ATOs), liquid oxygen (LOX) crews, safety observers, medical personnel, the landing signal officer.

- **RED SHIRTS**: Aviation ordnance crews.

JOHN DILLINGER AND THE WOMAN IN RED

July 20, 1934. The manhunt for John Dillinger has lasted two years. The nation, bitter and angry at banks, which have either failed or foreclosed on poor people's property, cheer the man who robs them. But FBI Director J. Edgar Hoover is not amused. He wants Dillinger and all the rest of the famous Depression-era criminals—Baby Face Nelson, Machine Gun Kelly, Ma Barker, Bonnie Parker, and Clyde Barrow—hunted down and killed, if necessary.

Melvin Purvis, agent in charge of the Dillinger manhunt, finally gets a break. A Romanian woman named Anna Sage calls from Chicago. Sage is a former madam with a criminal record, now a rooming house owner in Chicago. She has a wanted man staying at her place, she says—John Dillinger—and she'll give him up on two conditions: one, that she receive the reward money for his capture; and two, that Purvis help her out with the Immigration Department in their deportation hearings against her. Purvis agrees.

Sage says she will be accompanying Dillinger and his girlfriend, Polly Hamilton, to the movies on the night of July 22. They're going to see Clark Gable's new film, *Manhattan Melodrama*, at the Biograph Theater. She'll have on a bright red dress. When you see the dress, she said, the man with me will be Dillinger. (And don't shoot me, she seemed to be saying.)

Purvis and his men staked out the Biograph while the movie was playing. There were only a few of them who could identify Dillinger by sight, and there was talk that Dillinger had had his face altered by a plastic surgeon. So while they waited Purvis gave the agents this plan: Look for a lady in a red dress who'll be walking with a man and another woman. When you spot them, look over at me—if it really is Dillinger, I'll know it and I'll light a cigar.

Dillinger and his companions exited the theater an hour later. He didn't notice anything unusual on the street. Anna Sage walked a little ahead of the couple. They were easy to spot. Across the street, agent Melvin Purvis lit a cigar, and with that, the agents moved in, guns drawn. It was the guns Dillinger noticed first. He ran, but he didn't get far. Hit by five pistol shots, he died in a nearby alley.

In the newspapers the next day Dillinger was described in heroic terms, while Anna Sage, "the Woman in Red," was vilified as a betrayer. She didn't mind: She could take their scorn for what she was getting. But here is the irony: She got her reward money—five thousand dollars—but she was promptly deported back to Romania.

In LA, Clothes Make the Man

If you're a tourist who likes to visit big cities and get off the beaten path by strolling into unfamiliar neighborhoods, we suggest that you not do it in south central Los Angeles. And if you're bold enough to go, please don't put a bandana in your pocket or on your head—you don't know what you're getting into. You see, in this part of Los Angeles County wearing a certain color bandana or shirt, or sporting a particular brand of shoes, is a message, and could get you killed. Around these parts, clothing is a full-on symbol—an indication of whether you are in one of the Crips sets or one of the Bloods sets. Being Crips-dressed in a Bloods neighborhood, or vice versa, is just not a healthy thing to do. These rival gangs don't like each other much, and have been known to shoot at the mere sight of the other gang's colors. But, you say, it's just a bandana—it doesn't mean anything. You'd be right, anywhere but here. Here, you're wrong.

Basically, the message is this: If you wear blue, or a blue bandana, or call someone "cuzz," or wear British Knight shoes (BK equals Blood Killas), you're looking like a Crip. If you wear red, or a red bandana, you're looking like a Blood.

Our advice? Wear a tux.

Tying One On

When it's time to buy a new necktie, most modern men do not become obsessed about it. Faced with hundreds of options in the clothing store, they'll pick a pattern, a color, or a stripe, and they're done. But men used to be more particular and conscious of their tie choices, because all those stripes and colors and objects actually had meanings—meanings that important men in society understood very well. By wearing a certain tie, you told others "in the know" a lot about yourself. You would not have worn a midnight blue tie with brass crowns, for example, unless you really had been in the Royal Navy. You would not have worn a black tie adorned with yellow crocuses unless you really had attended Magdalen College, Cambridge. To be caught wearing the tie of a fraternity to which you did not belong would be the height of embarrassment. Ties were membership cards indicating to other men where you went to school, what regiment you belonged to, what club you belonged to, or what trade you were in.

Today those origins are lost on all but the most traditional men. Here are a few common patterns and what they originally meant:

- **A NAVY BLUE TIE WITH A GOLD, RED, AND SILVER CREST:** You went to Oxford.

- **A NAVY BLUE TIE WITH GOLD AND BLUE STRIPES:** You're a member of the Yorkshire County Cricket Club, founded in 1863.

- **ALTERNATING DIAGONAL STRIPES OF FUCHSIA, PURPLE, GREEN, AND COPPER:** You're a member of the Eton Ramblers.

- **A RED TIE WITH DIAGONAL WHITE STRIPES:** You're a member of the Duke of Wellington's Regiment.

- **A BLACK TIE WITH BLUE DIAGONAL STRIPES:** You're an Old Etonian, a graduate of Eton College, founded in the year 1440 by Henry VI.

- **AN INDIGO BLUE TIE WITH A SILVER DIAGONAL STRIPE:** You're an Old Boy from Harrow, just like Winston Churchill.

- **A TIE WITH GREEN, BLUE, AND YELLOW STRIPES:** You're a proud veteran of the Burmese Rifles.

6:

WATCH CAREFULLY . . . VERY CAREFULLY

TELEVISION—the greatest one-way messaging system ever devised! You can't have a conversation with it, but the inflow of sight-and-sound information is so deep and so satisfying that it is the most common global experience in human history. One could argue that television sends messages—secret or not—nonstop. What are commercials, after all, but signals that work on the mind in subtle psychological ways? Love it or hate it, television has been a medium for a variety of secret messages. Some are in front of the camera, some behind.

THE STORY OF JEREMIAH DENTON

You may recognize the name Jeremiah Denton. He was a senator from Alabama from 1981 to 1987, but that's probably not how you remember him. Most people will remember him from an appearance he made on television on May 17, 1966. He was not a television star, nor was he a politician, and he most certainly would have avoided this appearance if he could have. But he couldn't. He was a prisoner of war, held captive by the North Vietnamese.

Commander Denton was a Navy pilot who had been shot down during a mission over Thanh Hoa in 1965. For the next seven years he was battered, beaten, and put in solitary confinement at several prison camps around Hanoi. Being the senior POW at these camps, Commander Denton was constantly pressured by the Vietnamese, through torture and deprivation, to publicly "confess" his crimes and acknowledge the "criminal actions" of the United States. This was a propaganda coup he was not going to provide.

Finally forced in front of a television camera in May 1966 by the North Vietnamese, Denton used quick thinking and courage to turn the tables on his captors by using Morse Code in an ingenious way. The beauty of Morse Code has always been its elegant simplicity. The code can be communicated by any modality that can be varied into two states—on/off, up/down, open/closed, bright/dim, left/right, and so on, where one state represents a "dot" and the other represents a "dash." That means that you don't need a radio to send Morse; virtually anything will do—signal flags, mirrors, whistling, clapping hands, or thumps on an oil drum. All an inventive person needs is the code itself to communicate with others. Staring into the camera's lens, the haggard Denton came up with a plan. He mouthed the words the guards told him to say, but his eyes told a different story. They blinked, as if bothered by the television lights. And as they did, a pattern could be discerned. Pentagon observers suddenly sat bolt upright in their chairs. It was Morse Code, and the word Denton was blinking with his eyes sent a chill up their spines, and told the world for the first time what was happening to the American captives . . . T-O-R-T-U-R-E.

CAROL BURNETT'S EAR PROBLEM

The television comedienne Carol Burnett nearly always ended her shows and specials alone at stage front, facing the audience (and her millions of fans at home watching on TV) and singing, "I'm so glad we had this time together . . ." It was a nice touch, personal and warm, and people loved it. But were you among those who noticed that she tugged on her right earlobe at this point in the show every night? It was easy to miss, but sure enough, if you watched carefully you would see that Burnett would tilt her head and tug her earlobe every time. Some people thought it was a nervous tic; others thought she was doing it subconsciously. Still others thought she might have an ear problem. But Burnett confessed that it was simply a secret message she had worked out with her grandmother, who was watching the TV. What was the message? What else—"I love you!"

CAPTAIN MIDNIGHT

Most American kids of the 1950s era got their first exposure to the concept of secret messages from a television show called *Captain Midnight*. The television show evolved from a radio show broadcast by the Mutual Network in the 1940s, which itself was the follow-on of a show called *The Air Adventures of Jimmie Allen*, first broadcast in 1938 on WGN in Chicago. The sponsor of the Mutual show was Ovaltine, which had just dropped its sponsorship of the *Little Orphan Annie Show*. On the verge of war, the company was looking for a more heroic character with which to associate its product.

The television show was a big hit and was among the first shows to offer premiums to its young viewers. If you became a member of the Secret Squadron (after you had sent in lots of foil Ovaltine tops as proof of purchase), you would receive a magazine, decoder badges, decoder rings, pins, and other trinkets. These weren't just membership tokens; they were actually used as part of the show. Part of the story line for each show involved the sending of a secret message on the Captain Midnight Code-a-Graph. Kids at home could use their decoder rings to decipher the secret message.

This was one of television's first successful cross promotions—good for the show because kids flocked to see the messages and good for Ovaltine because the gimmick moved lots of product.

Captain Midnight's decoder badge had the password "Cobralhofa" on it. This ten-letter word was used to indicate that secret messages sent to Captain Midnight by his pal Chuck were coded so that the message could be revealed by reading every tenth word. Consider these two letters to the Captain from Chuck, who had been captured by the evil Ivan Shark, in which he tries to indicate Shark's hiding place: "Hello Captain Midnight. This is your last chance to come to an agreement with Ivan Shark. Please think it over. If you do not agree, this will be the bridge that will separate us forever. You should do the right thing. The thing that will surely bring us together at last . . ." And, "Hello Captain Midnight and everybody. Please do not delay long. Fly where Ivan Shark says. I will not be home again if you refuse. To do all these things on my account is a lot, I know. Remember that flying to Ivan Shark's direction just as straight as an arrow is essential . . ." By reading every tenth word, Captain Midnight knew where Chuck was held captive (and so did a nation of children): "Come over bridge, right at Long home, on Flying Arrow."

By the way, it has been long enough now that those decoder rings have achieved collector status. A Captain Midnight decoder ring in good condition will today bring five hundred dollars at auction.

7:

IT'S ALL SUBLIMINAL

YOU MAY BE RECEIVING secret messages without even knowing it. That's what skittish neuroscientists have been saying since the 1950s, when it came to their attention that human behavior could be surreptitiously manipulated with words and pictures on television screens. But human beings also send secret messages that they're not aware of. Just beneath the threshold of awareness, human beings are signaling all sorts of things to other people and animals who are attuned to the signals.

PERSUASION SCIENCE

Vance Packard's 1957 book *The Hidden Persuaders* made all of America suddenly suspicious of the radio and television shows they were enjoying. Packard introduced the idea that advertisers were influencing buying habits by subliminal means—that is, persuading by sending messages that arrived underneath the level of conscious awareness. Was it really possible, they wondered?

Exhibit A was the work of a motivational researcher named James Vicary. In a Fort Lee, New Jersey, movie theater in 1956, Vicary claimed that he had increased sales of Coca-Cola by 18 percent and popcorn by 58 percent by splicing a message into feature films. The message was not noticeable as the film was being shown, but it was there, nonetheless. What was the message? "Eat popcorn, drink Coke."

Whether the message really caused the sales increases is open for debate. Vicary himself thought not. "It was a gimmick," he said. Even if his "gimmick" had worked with advertisers, the public reaction to it would have kept the technique from being employed. Not surprisingly, research has since shown that people feel that subliminal advertising is not only unethical, but frightening in its many implications.

Communicating on a subliminal level, however, is far from over. While messages no longer flash on the movie screen, advertisers have studied communication stimuli so thoroughly that they can with confidence craft a message that subliminally resonates in the mind without using so much as a word. How do they do that? By using tools as common as color. Colors do more than attract attention: They communicate. Red, for example, subliminally tells us that a food product tastes good. Yellow is a very close second in this communication, and the two work wonderfully together (now you know why you have supernatural cravings for a Big Mac at McDonald's!). Proof? Look no further than your local supermarket to see how powerful these colors are. In fact, almost all of the dominant brand names in each of the "rich-tasting" categories of food products use red as a major color element on their labels or their packages. Campbell's soup cans? Red. Coca-Cola? Also red. Marlboro cigarettes? Red. KFC? Red again.

Green is another color that delivers a powerful secret communication. Green on a cigarette pack always means menthol, which, in turn, means "cool." On the other hand, green on a label of a prepared food product usually connotes low calories, or that it is a vegetable.

But there is much more to the subliminal messages of advertising and persuasion than color alone. Advertisers also study and craft the hidden "themes" within an ad. Thematic perceptions, as they are called, are powerful subliminal communicators and are ever-present. Madison Avenue holds that every ad communicates on two levels. The first is the rational or the literal level. Let's say an advertisement has a photograph of a man sitting at a desk. On the literal level, there is a man, a desk, and the man is sitting. But depending on the angle of his chin, or his posture, or the type of shirt he has on, we read certain themes into the photo—themes that go well beyond the literal elements. These are on the second level of communication, the thematic perceptions. If his chin is low we may read that he is depressed. If he has on a sport shirt we may think he is athletic or wealthy or, if it's obvious that he's in the office, that he's the owner or president of the firm, or a powerful person (who else gets to wear a sport shirt to the office?). There will be an altogether different thematic communication if he is leaning forward or leaning backward; with an elbow on the table; with both hands clasped; if he is looking into the camera or off-camera, and so on.

Look at an ad in your favorite magazine and see for yourself. Tobacco advertisers, pharmaceutical drug advertisers, and other advertisers in highly regulated industries are particularly reliant on these thematic elements. These advertisers are restricted in what they can say in their copy, but not in what their ads can say in your head. In fact, there are probably more thematic communications at work than literal ones. No surprise, then, that advertisers pay keen attention to this. While they may not flash messages on the movie screen anymore, they continue to carefully build thematic communication into every ad they create, leaving no opportunity missed for important subliminal messaging to occur, with or without our knowledge.

THE MESSAGE IS . . . I'M SCARED!

The prevailing wisdom among California surfers of the 1970s and 1980s concerning sharks was this: If a shark was swimming near you or at you, you tried not to show fear. Fear, they thought, could be sensed by the shark, and would precipitate an attack if it was too pronounced. Today, shark experts scoff at that idea. An attack will occur, they say, simply because the shark perceives you as food. But sharks do, in fact, have the ability to sense fear, in fish and humans. They have keen sensory organs along their sides and at the snout, which enable them to sense the electrical stimuli emitted by the body when muscles contract. The appearance of a large shark at close range would certainly cause the brain to become agitated and fearful, which would engage the hypothalamus gland, which would send a "fight or flight" signal to the muscles, which would contract involuntarily. A shark has the ability to sense this electro-chemical-muscular event. And it turns out that other animals do, too. Dogs, especially, have been known to react to the electrical emission from the body that is generated by strong emotion such as fear. So, in effect, it is true that the human body sends out secret messages of which it is not cognitively aware.

The anthropologist Desmond Morris, among others, also reminds us that the body constantly sends subliminal messages, especially of a sexual nature. The pupils of the eyes, for example, which normally dilate according to the amount of light passing through, can dilate beyond the normal size when the brain perceives something it likes. It could be a potential mate, or a precious gem, or a beloved relative, but the pupils will dilate strongly when the brain is emotionally aroused.

This fact can be exploited by perceptive salesmen who can occasionally "read" the eyes, which subliminally express an overwhelming desire to purchase something. Conversely, it is said that Oriental jade merchants always wear sunglasses, so as to hide their eagerness to purchase valuable samples from jade producers.

BETTER BY YOU, BETTER THAN ME

This was the name of a song on the 1978 album *Stained Class* by the British heavy metal band Judas Priest. It was on this song that the band was alleged, in a 1989 lawsuit by two sets of Nevada parents, to have subliminally recorded the words "Do it," which the plaintiffs further alleged was the trigger that led to the suicide deaths of their sons in 1985.

The Nevada trial became one of the landmark cases involving the existence or nonexistence of subliminal communication, or the ability of subthreshold communication to influence behavior. Plaintiffs' experts argued in the affirmative, that the words "Do it" had been placed subliminally on the song; that its intent was to push people to commit suicide; and that, in fact, two young men had been brainwashed into committing that act. The band's attorneys argued that the band had placed no such words on the song, and repeated listening to all twenty-four tracks of the song by the court confirmed this fact. Further, they argued that even if the words had been present, the words themselves did not have the inherent power to move anyone to such extreme behavior. In this second argument lay the important legal ruling, which had immense implications for all recording artists: Did subliminal messages exist or not, and did they have the power to influence behavior?

Judge Jerry Carr Whitehead ultimately ruled for the defendants, saying, "The scientific research presented does not establish that subliminal stimuli, even if perceived, may precipitate conduct of this magnitude."

The law, then, does not recognize the existence of subliminal secret messages. And the creator of the idea, James "Eat popcorn, drink Coke" Vicary, says it does not work. But popular opinion says it does. Time Warner even created a computer game called Endorfun that plays on this perception. The program contains positive, life-enhancing subliminal messages. The game's motto? "Play more. Feel better."

10-2-4

The new soft drink tasted pretty good, but it had a funny name: Dr Pepper. And the logo had three mysterious numbers on it—10-2-4. What did that mean? Those numbers were part of an advertising campaign that was so clever it lasted fifty years. It started like this: A 1927 study on human fatigue seemed to suggest that a person's energy level dropped to its lowest points at 10:30 A.M., 2:30 P.M., and 4:30 P.M. This was a fact that the advertising agency Tracy-Locke-Dawson could use to the advantage of its client, Dr Pepper. From that point on, and for the next fifty years, Dr Pepper's advertising and bottle designs included the numbers 10-2-4, which stayed mysterious only until one heard the reasoning behind it. And if you believed it (and a lot of people did), then you had a terrific reason to drink Dr Pepper three times per day. The slogan said it all: "Three good times to enjoy life more."

Secret Slogans

Do you remember the logo LS/MFT? It adorned the side panel of a package of Lucky Strike cigarettes and was also used in the product's advertising. In the beginning, no one knew what it meant, and that was the point. It was like a puzzle. Soon those in the know knew that it meant "Lucky Strike Means Fine Tobacco."

More prevalent, at least for about a decade, were roads signs with these amusing poems. Can you recognize the product they advertised?

> IN CUPID'S LITTLE
> BAG OF TRIX
> HERE'S THE ONE
> THAT CLIX
> WITH CHIX

> WE DON'T
> KNOW HOW
> TO SPLIT AN ATOM
> BUT AS TO WHISKERS
> LET US AT 'EM

> IF YOU WANT
> A HEARTY SQUEEZE
> GET OUR
> FEMALE
> ANTI-FREEZE

The answer? Burma Shave.

READING YOU LIKE A BOOK

Let's say you play poker once a week with the guys. You're pretty good; you usually leave the table with more money than you came with. Since the local boys can't stay with you, could you, you wonder, take your game to the championship tables in Las Vegas? If you got a lucky run of cards, couldn't that be possible? The answer is no. The casinos in Vegas are littered with the hollowed-out cadavers of men who thought they could roll with the big boys. Why couldn't they win? Didn't they know the game and the odds well enough? They probably did; not knowing the game was not why they lost. They lost because their bodies sent secret messages they couldn't control. They lost because Doyle "Texas Dolly" Brunson, Phil Hellmuth, Johnny Chan, and all the other professional poker players knew when the bluff was on and when they had winning cards.

How did they know? They simply watched the amateurs play. After a few hands the experts can find everyone's "tells." A tell is a movement, a sound, a twitch, a scratching of the nose, a whistle—any involuntary action that occurs when a player has a good hand, or has a bad hand but plays to bluff. Most of the time the player is not aware of his own tells. But the pros are. When John Doe over there starts lightly whistling "When the Saints Go Marching In," everyone knows he's got a full house. He does it every time!

Poker wannabes have known about tells for a long time, and most go into the big games determined to control themselves, to not reveal anything by their subliminal behavior. But that is the nature of subliminal behavior. It occurs without awareness. In the stress of a game, at important moments, when there are thousands of dollars at stake, the amateur will show his tell, and the pros take advantage of the moment.

No one is better at this than poker super-pro Johnny Chan. At the pro level, everyone has about the same level of math skill and the same knowledge of odds. What separates them is absolute self-control, the kind that disguises strategy, and the ability to peer across the table and spot a tell, or in the absence of a tell, have a spooky, unerring instinct about what cards the other player is holding. Chan has done this so often that some people feel he has made a Robert Johnson–style pact with the devil. They say there is no other way to explain it. Chan disagrees. He says that a careful observation of the opponent's body and involuntary movement will tell him all he needs to know. At crunch time, he says, a player who decides to bluff may believe it in his mind, but in his heart he is unsure. And when that happens, it shows. The physiognomy, he says, changes character and exhibits weakness. And then Chan has the upper hand in the showdown, and generally walks away with the money. The opponent sits and wonders just what he did that Chan spotted, and he'll never know.

8 :

SPANKY GOES TO BUCKEYE

SENSITIVE INFORMATION sometimes has to be transmitted by radio or walkie-talkie over public airwaves. When this involves people, the only way to disguise the content of the message is by creating codenames. Codenames are simply an agreement among the communicators that false names are to be used instead of real names. The substitutions must be explicitly understood by all parties to be effective, and therefore must be committed to paper or memory.

THE CENTRAL AMERICA

A classic example of this can be found in the story of the underwater discovery of the sunken side-wheeler *Central America.*

If anything marks the competitive, backbiting world of underwater salvagers, it is intrigue. With tactics almost as sophisticated as those developed by the CIA, treasure hunters will go to any lengths to learn where a sunken ship might have gone down.

No stranger to this world was a remarkable man by the name of Tommy Thompson. Thompson wanted to find the wreckage of the

Central America, which went down at the height of the California Gold Rush 130 years ago. If he found it, he and his investors stood to make hundreds of millions of dollars. But where was the *Central America?* Through meticulous research, Thompson pinpointed a searchable area of ocean bottom two hundred miles off the coast of North Carolina in nine thousand feet of water. Using a sonar "fish" dragged by his research vessel, he and his team scanned the entire area until they saw something.

Thompson, though, ran a tight ship, and those weighing the sonar readouts were given specific instructions about what to say if they spotted something that might be of interest to Thompson. They were never to use the words *"Central America"* or "shipwreck" or "ship" or even "treasure." Then what would describe a possible sunken ship? "We have a possible cultural deposit here."

Incidentally, when the *Central America* finally succumbed to the heavy seas, her captain sent one last message. He fired three rockets straight down toward the water. With this, the captains of the rescue vessels sadly knew the truth: the *Central America* was now going under. If the rockets had been fired into the air, the meaning would have been different—the ship still had a chance.

Secret Service Codenames

The Secret Service is perhaps one of the most prolific users of codenames and phrases. Its agents guard and protect the president of the United States and his family and other high-ranking government officials. They communicate as unobtrusively as possible with each other, but they have to do it over radio frequencies that could be easily intercepted. To safeguard their information from eavesdroppers the Secret Service has developed a glossary of codenames. Some of these names have been in use for years. Others are developed as needed. Here is a list of Secret Service codenames for a wide variety of people, places, and things. ("Spanky," by the way, is Ronald Reagan, while "Buckeye" was the presidential retreat, Camp David):

ACROBAT	ANDREWS AIR FORCE BASE, MARYLAND
BAMBOO	PRESIDENTIAL MOTORCADE
BANDBOX	SECRET SERVICE WHITE HOUSE UNIT
BIRDSEYE	DEPARTMENT OF STATE
BRIMSTONE	REAGAN RANCH, CALIFORNIA
BUCKEYE	CAMP DAVID, MARYLAND
CEMENT MIXER	WHITE HOUSE SITUATION ROOM
CHANDELIER	DEPARTMENT OF STATE
CLOVERLEAF	VICE-PRESIDENT'S RESIDENCE
COACH HOUSE	DULLES AIRPORT, WASHINGTON, D.C.
COBWEB	VICE-PRESIDENT'S OFFICE
COMPANION	BLAIR HOUSE, WASHINGTON, D.C.
CURBSIDE	NATIONAL AIRPORT, WASHINGTON, D.C.
DRIFTWOOD	CARTER HOME, GEORGIA
ELM	CAMP DAVID, MARYLAND
FIRESIDE	SECRETARY OF STATE'S RESIDENCE
HILL TOP	TREASURY DEPARTMENT
HUDSON	NIXON OFFICE, NEW YORK
PAVILLION	VICE-PRESIDENT'S OFFICE
PENINSULA	NEW SENATE OFFICE BUILDING
PINCUSHION	RAYBURN OFFICE BUILDING, WASHINGTON, D.C.
PORK CHOP	OLD SENATE OFFICE BUILDING
PROFESSOR	LONGWORTH BUILDING, WASHINGTON, D.C.
PUNCH BOWL	CAPITOL BUILDING
RIDGELINE	REAGAN RESIDENCE, CALIFORNIA
RINGSIDE	MADISON SQUARE GARDEN, NEW YORK
ROADHOUSE	WALDORF ASTORIA, NEW YORK
SANDSTONE	REAGAN RESIDENCE, CALIFORNIA
STORE ROOM	TRUMAN LIBRARY, MISSOURI
STORM KING	NIXON RESIDENCE, NEW JERSEY
TOOL ROOM	VICE-PRESIDENT'S OFFICE
TOWER	ANDREWS AIR FORCE BASE, MARYLAND
VOLCANO	LBJ RANCH, TEXAS

OBJECTS AND EVENTS

ANGEL	AIR FORCE ONE
CARGO	MRS. MONDALE'S CAR
CAROUSEL	AIR FORCE TWO
CHARIOT	MONDALE VEHICLE
DOG POUND	PRESS AIRCRAFT
MARINE ONE	PRESIDENT'S HELICOPTER
MARINE TWO	VICE-PRESIDENT'S HELICOPTER
SATURN	VICE-PRESIDENT'S AIRCRAFT
STAGECOACH	PRESIDENT'S LIMOUSINE
WHEELS DOWN	PRESIDENTIAL AIRCRAFT HAS LANDED
WHEELS UP	PRESIDENTIAL AIRCRAFT HAS TAKEN OFF

PEOPLE

CALICO	ELEANOR MONDALE
CAMEO	JOAN MONDALE
CANNONBALL	REAR ADMIRAL J. A. CHANEY
CAVALIER	WALTER MONDALE
CEDAR	MENACHEM BEGIN
CLAM CHOWDER	RON NESSEN
CLAW HAMMER	ALEXANDER HAIG
COPPERTONE	ROSE KENNEDY
DAILY	PRINCE CHARLES
DANCER	ROSALYNN CARTER
DASHER	JIMMY CARTER
DEACON	JIMMY CARTER
DRAGON	WALTER MONDALE
DYNAMO	AMY CARTER
EAGLE	BILL CLINTON
EVERGREEN	HILLARY CLINTON
FADEAWAY	SECRETARY OF STATE
FENCING MASTER	SECRETARY OF TREASURY
FINLEY	SECRETARY OF DEFENSE
FIREPLUG	SECRETARY OF LABOR

FISTFIGHT	SECRETARY OF HEW
FLAG DAY	SPEAKER, HOUSE OF REPRESENTATIVES
FLIVVER	WILLIAM FRENCH SMITH
FLOTUS	THE FIRST LADY
FLYING FISH	SECRETARY OF THE INTERIOR
FOOTPRINT	SENATOR STROM THURMOND
HALO	POPE JOHN PAUL II
HAWKEYE	Z. BRZEZINSKI
INSTRUCTOR	EUGENE MCCARTHY
KITTYHAWK	QUEEN ELIZABETH II
LANCER	JOHN F. KENNEDY
LOCK MASTER	JIMMY CARTER
LOTUS PETAL	ROSALYNN CARTER
NAPOLEON	FRANK SINATRA
PASS KEY	GERALD FORD
PINAFORE	BETTY FORD
POTUS	PRESIDENT OF THE UNITED STATES
RAINBOW	NANCY REAGAN
RAWHIDE	RONALD REAGAN
REDFERN	QUEEN ELIZABETH II
REDWOOD	GARY HART
RHYME	MAUREEN REAGAN
RIBBON	PATTI REAGAN DAVIS
RIDDLER	MICHAEL REAGAN
SCORECARD	DAN QUAYLE
SEARCHLIGHT	RICHARD NIXON
SHEEPSKIN	GEORGE BUSH
SNAPSHOT	HOWARD BAKER
SNOWBANK	BARBARA BUSH
SNOWSTORM	GEORGE BUSH
SPANKY	RONALD REAGAN
SPRINGTIME	MAMIE EISENHOWER
STARLIGHT	PAT NIXON
STRAWBERRY	ROSEMARY WOODS
SUNBURN	TED KENNEDY

SUNDANCE	ETHEL KENNEDY
SUNSHINE	MARILYN QUAYLE
SUPERVISOR	DAN QUAYLE
THUNDER	JESSE JACKSON
TIMBERWOLF	GEORGE BUSH
TRANQUILITY	BARBARA BUSH
TUMBLER	GEORGE W. BUSH, JR.
UNICORN	PRINCE CHARLES
VICTORIA	LADYBIRD JOHNSON
VOLUNTEER	LYNDON JOHNSON
WELCOME	J. R. HALDEMAN
WHALEBOAT	RON ZIEGLER
WISDOM	J. EHRLICHMAN
WOODCUTTER	HENRY KISSINGER

THE VENONA PROJECT

On February 1, 1943, the U.S. Army's Signal Intelligence Service (later to become the National Security Agency) began a secret program codenamed "The Venona Project," which examined encrypted Soviet diplomatic communications that had been intercepted and accumulated by the SIS.

The intelligence haul was an unorganized collection of thousands of Soviet diplomatic telegrams that had been sent in code from Moscow to certain of its diplomatic missions and from those missions to Moscow.

From the very beginning the analysis of these telegrams was arduous. It wasn't until the summer of 1946, after World War II, that the Service could read portions of KGB messages that had been sent between the KGB Residency in New York and Moscow Center. With the now-celebrated cryptanalyst Meredith Gardner leading the way to cryptographic breakthroughs, in late summer of '46 they decoded a discussion of clandestine KGB activity in Latin America. On December 13, 1946, Gardner was able to read a KGB message that discussed the U.S. presidential election campaign of 1944. Soon after came a real bombshell: They decoded a two-year-old message in which were listed the names of the leading scientists working on the Manhattan Project, the supposedly airtight nuclear weapons program. It was then that the full extent and intent of Soviet espionage in the United States was understood.

A tantalizing aspect of this message traffic was the Soviet use of code and cover names. The Venona Project turned up hundreds of them, most being codenames for KGB agents, including ANTENNA and LIBERAL, both later identified as code names for Julius Rosenberg. (One message mentioned that LIBERAL's wife was named "Ethel.")

The following are examples of cover names discovered from the Venona cache:

- **KAPITAN** was the code name for President Roosevelt.

- **ANTENNA** or **LIBERAL** was the codename for Julius Rosenberg.

- **BABYLON** was the codename for San Francisco.

- **THE BANK** was the codename for the U.S. Department of State.

- **ARSENAL** was the codename for the U.S. War Department.

- **ENORMOZ** was the codename for the Manhattan Project.

- **ANTON** was the codename for Leonid Krasnikov, KGB chief of atomic espionage in the KGB's New York City office.

9:

IN THE BOOT

A S YOUNG AMERICA FOUGHT to break away from British colonial rule, the need for clandestine messaging was great. The British, after all, were on American soil and mingling every day with the enemy. Their proximity and their vigilance prompted General George Washington to create a sophisticated network of spies whose exploits helped win the war. These two stories from the Revolutionary War demonstrate that the cost of failed espionage is high, indeed.

THE TRAITOR'S CODE

In May 1779 American general Benedict Arnold, stung by perceived slights from the Continental Congress and pressed for money in his private life, quietly set in motion a plan to betray his country. He indicated to Joseph Stansbury, a Tory friend from Philadelphia, his intention, as Stansbury later recalled, of "opening his services to the commander-in-chief of the British army." Through various intermediaries Arnold's message found its way to Major John Andre, the young aide to the British commander, General Sir Henry Clinton.

With Clinton's blessing, Major Andre took charge of this clandestine recruiting coup. In his return letter to Stansbury, Andre indicated how welcome Arnold's help would be, and dropped hints of rewards and positions that would come Arnold's way for services rendered. His letter was more concise concerning how he proposed that he and Arnold would communicate secretly. It seems Major Andre fancied himself a master spy and a student of the black arts, and he leaped at this chance to exercise his predilection for coded letters.

Andre specified that they would funnel all messages through Stansbury, and that they would use a number code based on a "key." The key was a book—Volume One of *Blackstone's Commentaries on the Laws of England*. To write his message, Arnold was instructed to think of his first word—let's say it was the word "dear"—and then find the word "dear" somewhere in the aforementioned book. He would transcribe the page number on which it was found, the line number, and the position of the word in the line, rendering a three-number sequence, such as 157-30-9. His correspondent, who also had the Blackstone book, would simply turn to page 157, find line number 30, and count over to the ninth word. That was the first word in the message.

This key-book method of encipherment was an old chestnut in the spy business even in 1779. But it was effective and very safe. It still is today. As long as the key book is known only to the correspondents, their coded messages are unbreakable. Variations on this method were still being used in World War II when the "keys" were famous poems.

But there was a problem for Arnold. It lay in the cumbersome and labor-intensive diligence needed to send even the simplest message. By all accounts the *Commentaries* was a large, heavy book, and Arnold discounted the system immediately. After the first attempt his correspondence usually was written in plain English, but signed with pseudonyms such as "Monk" (a direct reference to George Monk, a general in Oliver Cromwell's army who rejoined the royalist side after Cromwell's death), "Moore," and "Gustavus." For his part, Andre signed his letters, "John Anderson."

It took a year and a half of correspondence to get to the moment when Arnold had the guarantees he wanted of payment of thirty thousand dollars from the British, and the British were assured that Arnold would surrender the American fort at West Point, New York, to them. But in the final days before the British attempt on West Point, Major Andre, the mastermind of the whole affair, was captured near Tarrytown, New York, carrying documents that implicated Arnold. This man who dabbled in spycraft had committed two monumental blunders—one, he had been captured with incriminating documents stuck in his boot; two, he was out of uniform. He had been ordered by General Clinton not to take off his British uniform, but, ironically, he was persuaded to do so by . . . Benedict Arnold. Now, by a cruel twist of fate, the soldier who played as a spy was caught as a spy. The penalty for this was death. But wait: Alexander Hamilton had an idea. Let's exchange Major Andre, he proposed, for that traitor, Benedict Arnold. General Clinton reluctantly declined, as did George Washington. As sad as the decision made them both, there was no other way. Major Andre was hanged as a spy on October 2, 1780.

With this, Benedict Arnold's fate as a pariah on both sides of the Atlantic was sealed. The British had lost a well-loved and promising young officer, and what did they get in exchange? A crippled, middle-aged egomaniac who was roundly blamed for Andre's death. Arnold was shunned by the British army, never given a decent posting, and was rejected by London society. And in America, his name is still invoked as that of the most egregious traitor in history.

THE DEATH OF THE FIRST AMERICAN MARTYR

Young Nathan Hale, a nineteen-year-old Yale graduate, was teaching school in Connecticut in 1774, but like all the other young men in New England, he was burning with revolutionary fever. He yearned for a life under arms, and soon he joined the Seventh Connecticut Regiment.

After a year in service, Hale found himself arriving late one night to a meeting of officers in which General George Washington had expressed the need for a "volunteer of intelligence." Washington's desperate need was for spying in New York City. Until Hale entered the room, no one had volunteered to be Washington's spy. Hale stepped into the vacuum, volunteering immediately. As friends later reminded him of the dangers and the risk of dying in ignominy, Hale is said to have replied, "I wish to be useful, and every kind of service necessary to the public good becomes honorable by being necessary."

Despite having no training at all in the profession of espionage, Hale surrendered his uniform and took on civilian clothes. He took on the guise of his old trade, that of a Connecticut schoolmaster. He traveled down Long Island Sound by boat, and was put ashore at Oyster Bay, from where he would make his way into the city. Before setting off, he made arrangements with the boatman to pick him up in one week's time, on September 20, 1776. He would signal with a lantern from shore.

Hale's concept of intelligence was to observe, then to commit his observations to paper in Latin, which he assumed would be a good enough code language to survive a casual search. He was, after all, traveling as a teacher. But for additional security he decided to hide his papers in the soles of his shoes.

Having committed his thoughts to paper and hidden them away, Hale made his way back to Oyster Bay where he awaited his boat.

And there it was, gliding like a shadow in the dark night toward shore. Hale raised his lantern. But it was not his ship. It was a British frigate, coming ashore for water. Hale tried to flee but was caught. A search turned up the papers in his shoe. The Latin was easily translated by the British, and Hale's mission as a spy was revealed. He was taken aboard the frigate, which sailed immediately for British general William Howe's headquarters in New York.

Howe was in no mood for clemency, and there never was a trial. The general merely ordered Hale hanged the following morning. The ignominious death that his friends had foretold was about to happen. On the morning of September 22, 1776, Nathan Hale, twenty-one, was marched to a nearby orchard and hanged from an apple tree.

10:

IT IS HOT IN SUEZ

IT IS NO WONDER that code and espionage stories from World War II are still surfacing after fifty-five years. The sheer volume of them could never be contained in a single book. Code buffs consider the years of Nazi occupation of Europe the Golden Age, when codemakers and codebreakers achieved heroic stature, and their accomplishments truly did shape the course of world history.

Pound for pound there will never be such an assemblage of code geniuses as those gathered on both sides of the conflict from 1938 to 1945. Viewed in terms of an intellectual contest, this was the Super Bowl, the Big League of cryptography, and there weren't many days when staggeringly inventive work was not done.

But these were the years of amateur, make-do espionage, too, carried out by ordinary men and women with no cryptographic training at all. Some of the street-level codes and ruses they devised were as cunning and complex—and as ruthless—as anything devised by the professionals.

Here, then, are some secret message stories from World War II. For every one written here there are thousands more, of messages sent and received every day across every theater of war by people whose names we will never know.

Gone Fishing

During World War II, codebreakers on all sides were intercepting messages of every type—written, verbal (telephone and radio), telex, and so forth—almost hourly. The most important of these messages would ultimately find their way onto the desk of President Roosevelt, in the case of Americans, or that of Winston Churchill, in the case of the British.

If the Germans were listening to President Roosevelt's phone conversations with Winston Churchill, as some say they were, they must have been puzzled by a line from Roosevelt that came at the end of a tense 1944 discussion about war plans. To Churchill's question, "What are you going to do next?" Roosevelt replied, "I think I'll go fishing," which must have sounded amazingly nonchalant to the eavesdropping Germans. What they didn't know was that Roosevelt was letting Churchill know that he was going to read the recently intercepted and decoded messages from the German High Command, which came from the Ultra intercepts. The office staff at the White House had taken to calling them "fish."

Dutch Curtains

The story of Anne Frank and her family is perhaps the best known of the Holocaust stories, but during the years from 1939 to 1945 similar stories were played out all over Europe. In Holland, the tough and fearless Dutch Underground was a particularly tenacious foe of the Gestapo.

Many houses in Amsterdam, Haarlem, and other Dutch cities were rigged to shelter fugitive Jewish families, who hid in crawl spaces, in attics, behind false walls, and in basements. The very active and efficient Underground delivered food and clothing to these families daily, right under the noses of the Germans. How did they do it? Before entering the homes, Underground members would first look at the front of the house. If the bottom-floor window curtains were open, the house was safe to enter. If one side of the curtain was closed, that meant trouble. Either the house was being watched, or German soldiers had actually commandeered the house as a barracks.

In Haarlem, in 1944, a Jewish family of eight took shelter in a crawl space under the first floor of a house. No sooner had they squeezed in than a squad of German soldiers walked into the house and decided to live there. The Underground noticed. An Underground member, posing as a friend of the homeowner making a social call, entered the house and, while inside, managed to close a curtain halfway. Now no one would bring food to the house, but the family was stuck under the floorboards, and could make no noise, not even a cough. For a full week the Germans stayed, and the family persevered until they finally left. They emerged, famished and shaken, but alive—except for one. During the week, one of the family members had died, exhaling a last breath with the hands of the family over his mouth to cover the sound.

For the duration of the war, the Gestapo never caught on that the curtains in their own "homes" were being used to help the Underground—and that a half-closed curtain was a secret message that said, "Do not enter."

SINKING THE *BISMARCK*

KRKRX FLOTT ENCHE FANAN OKMM XXTOR PEDOT REFFE RACHT ERAUS XSCHI FFMAN OEVRI ERUNF AEHIG XWIRK AEMPF ENBIS ZURLE TZTEN GRANA TEXES LEBED ERFUE HRERX

No, it's not a language that you missed in school. The seeming gibberish above is a message that was sent fifty years ago using a secret machine dubbed Enigma. The message relates to one of the most dramatic chases in naval history. Developed by German cryptologists, Enigma was such a complex enciphering machine that the Germans thought it to be unbreakable, which, of course, was its undoing. Enigma was in fact broken even before America joined the war. The

German sentence you see above was generated by the Enigma machine, but it was read by the intelligence services with ease. No doubt they smiled when they got it. The message was intercepted in 1941 and marked the end of the most fabled of all sea hunts—the hunt for the German battleship *Bismarck*.

A little history is in order. The *Bismarck* dwarfed everything on the sea. Its guns were bigger than anything the British had, her armor was thicker than that of any ship before her, and her engines were the most powerful on the seas. If the Allies were to keep the sea lanes open, they had to sink the *Bismarck* before she dominated the North Atlantic.

In May 1941, the hunt was on. The *Bismarck* slipped out of port, past Norway and out toward the North Atlantic. Search planes leaped into the skies and began flying reconnaissance grids while British surface ships and submarines scoured the horizon for the first telltale signs. The British navy actually found her, but only at great cost. On May 24, in a naval duel with the battleship *Prince of Wales* and the battle cruiser *Hood*, *Bismarck* showed her terrible power, sinking the *Hood*.

The *Bismarck* was found, but she was every bit the ultimate dreadnought that the Allies feared her to be. Could she be sunk? The answer came on May 26. A frail, obsolete torpedo bomber called a Swordfish saw the ship, and the pilot bravely dropped his single torpedo into the Atlantic. The pilot watched as it churned toward the mighty ship, the torpedo looking smaller and smaller as it sped toward the target. The Bismarck deftly turned to evade the oncoming warhead of TNT, and it looked like a miss. And it almost was. In fact, if the torpedo had been a truer shot it would have blasted harmlessly against the ship's thick steel hull. Instead it nearly missed, hitting only the exposed rudders at the stern of the ship. But what a place to hit. The *Bismarck*'s rudders were jammed and the once-invincible ship was reduced to sailing helplessly in circles. Desperate, the German captain sent the message above in Enigma code. It says: "Commander-in-Chief Fleet to Naval Headquarters: Torpedo hit right aft. Ship unmaneuverable. We fight to the last shell. Long live the Führer."

She sank before sunset the next day, May 27.

THE BENT-LEG BEAM

KNICKEBEIN KLEVE IST AUF PUNKT FUNF DREI GRAD ZWEI VIER
MINUTEN NORD UND EINS GRAD WEST EINGERICHTET

Translation: "Bent-leg beam at Kleve is directed to the point 53° 24' N.
1° W."

With Enigma broken, intelligence was rolling in by the wheelbar-
row-full. There was too much, actually. Code clerks were barely man-
aging to keep up with the daily inflow of messages intercepted from
the various German commands. The message above was almost
thrown away, but at the last moment it raised a few eyebrows. What
was this "bent-leg beam"?

The intelligence was passed on to the appropriate authorities, who
also happened to be interested. They had been informed recently of a
conversation overheard between two German prisoners in which they
discussed a new radio beam capable of guiding bombers with new, un-
heard-of accuracy to their targets. At the time, they had laughed at
such braggadocio, but it was war and everything was noted just in case.

Had the prisoners been talking about this same bent-leg beam?

Radar was so new that no one truly appreciated its potential. Everyone understood that it could identify invading aircraft, but it wasn't yet
seen as a guidance tool. Experts were puzzled at such a possibility.
Why, they wondered, would the Germans want to resort to that kind of
scientific complexity when navigation by the stars could do just as
well? (Actually, it wasn't such an accurate way to navigate, particularly
under heavy clouds. In fact, the British had a terrible time finding their
way over Germany and consistently missed their bombing targets.)

Ridicule was just the sort of behavior that caught the eye of Prime
Minister Winston Churchill. Churchill was apprised of the message
and he was given the various theories of its meaning, but to his ear, dis-
missing the message sounded like just the sort of thing England would
later come to regret. Churchill didn't laugh off the idea of a guided
bomber at all. In fact, he insisted that a search for the beam be insti-
gated immediately.

An airplane equipped with sensitive receivers soon found it. Following its path, they quickly discovered its purpose. It passed directly over the Rolls-Royce factory at Derby, where engines for RAF fighters were manufactured! Had it not been discovered, German bombers would have flown the beam like a highway in the night, directly to their target.

Countermeasures to jam the beams were soon developed, at first employing jury-rigged diathermy machines borrowed from local hospitals. The code-breaking initiative that had turned the German Enigma machine into an Allied war asset, an initiative called Ultra, had achieved its first practical success.

An Unbreakable American Code

Who better than American codebreakers in World War II knew how vulnerable mechanical code machines were? After all, they had broken the Japanese and German cipher machines, enabling them to read and understand nearly all enemy communications traffic. When the idea emerged that perhaps human-to-human, spoken code language might be more secure than machines, they were receptive. But what language? There was early interest in several Native American languages—Choctaw, Chippewa, Commanche, Oneida. As rare as they were, they were discarded because there was some evidence that German foreign exchange students had studied those languages. But there was one language they didn't know—Navajo. The Navajo people were much more isolated than most other tribes, unlikely to have visitors, and their language was much more difficult to learn. In fact, it was nearly impossible for even other Native American tribes to understand. Each syllable of the Navajo language means something, and the pronunciation has to be exact. The modulation of tones—so slight that nonspeakers cannot hear the difference—is critical to understanding. It was estimated that in 1941 only a handful of people outside the tribe had even rudimentary knowledge of its vocabulary.

Of special interest to military planners was the fact that Navajo was a spoken, not a written, language. This led them to a belief that Navajo might be the perfect radio sending and receiving language.

A cadre of some two hundred young Navajo men was recruited into this specialized service. Placed in various Marine radio companies, they served valiantly, especially in the Pacific Theater, where their radio messages made a critical difference on Iwo Jima, Guam, and other jungle locations. Ironically, it was not Navajo that these men were speaking to each other, as most people believe. Before being inserted into actual combat situations, the Navajo men took the time to create an all-new code language with Navajo root words. They created new words for over twenty basic military terms, and an alphabet code that was changeable from day to day, to prevent the Japanese from cracking their code through word frequency charts. The letter "a," for example, could be wol-la-chee (ant), be-las-saaa (apple), or tse-nihl (axe). By the time they were deployed overseas, the Navajo were speaking an entirely new language. Not even a native Navajo speaker could have deciphered the full meaning of their transmissions. As an American codebreaker said after a training test, "It sounded like gibberish. We couldn't even transcribe it, much less break it!"

THE DOLL LADY

Velvalee Dickinson wasn't a bad person. She was just sympathetic to Japanese causes, and was a bit naïve about the illegality of passing information about the comings and goings of American warships to the man at the Buenos Aires address. But it was 1943 and there was a war on; she understood her delicate position well enough to know that she should be careful. So she disguised her information in a code she herself invented.

It all started when she and her husband had lived on the coast of California before the war. There they had made friends with a number of Japanese couples and even some Japanese naval officers. When her husband got sick, Velvalee Dickinson's world came to an end. The medical bills wiped out her savings, and in the end it didn't save her husband's life. Broke, dispirited, and now alone, she took solace in the only thing she still loved—her large doll collection.

That's when the nice Japanese man came to see her. For a sum of money so large it seemed unreal, she agreed to tell him about the American ships—the ones coming in, the ones going out, what kind of ships they were, things like that. It didn't seem like such a hard thing to do, and besides, she liked the Japanese.

Then the war started, and the money helped her move to New York, which the Japanese didn't mind at all. She opened a doll shop on Madison Avenue and sent reports when she could about the ships in New York Harbor. She sent them where the Japanese man told her to—an address in Buenos Aires, Argentina. Her letters used her doll business as her source code. If she wrote that she had "three new dolls," her contact knew three ships had come into port. When she wrote of one doll as "an old Irish fisherman with a net over his back" it referred to an aircraft carrier. The secret messages were then sealed in ordinary business envelopes and mailed. For a return address, she used various names and addresses from real correspondence that came into her shop.

The whole setup would have gone undetected, but the Japanese abandoned the Buenos Aires address and forgot to inform Dickinson. Her letters stacked up in the Buenos Aires post office and were soon marked "undeliverable" and returned to the addresses on the envelopes. All over America people started getting mail back that they had never sent in the first place. On opening the letters, they read odd messages about dolls, and found their own names forged at the bottom. It didn't take long before the FBI got involved, and it was relatively simple to trace the letters back to Velvalee Dickinson, the little old lady in the doll shop. She was arrested as she was taking the last eight thousand dollars of her Japanese bounty out of the bank. Her simple plan would have worked if she had not gone to the trouble of including a return address on her letters. Though caught red-handed, she was a sympathetic character and received only a ten-year prison sentence for her crime. Others of another sex or at another time might have been hanged from a gallows.

A CROSSWORD SPY?

By May 1944 Allied plans for the invasion of Europe were nearing completion. The unimaginably complex logistics of landing several armies' worth of men and materiel had been worked out in strict secrecy, with codenames for all operations given only to key personnel. Although military planners were not so naïve as to think the Nazis did not expect some kind of invasion, they still felt the element of surprise—where, when, how many men—was an important factor in the enterprise. It was crucial to safeguard these plans from the enemy's intelligence resources.

It seemed to be working. German commanders were hopelessly at odds on where and when the invasion would come, and were busily putting mines as far off base as the Bay of Biscay, and reinforcing troops in unlikely places such as the Baltics and Norway.

How surprising was it, then, to notice the crossword puzzle in London's *Daily Telegraph* on Saturday, May 27, 1944? The clue read, "but some bigwig like this has stolen some of it at times," yielding the answer, OVERLORD, which we all know from our history was the codename for the entire D-Day invasion! Someone at MI5 must have fallen off his chair! Scrambling investigators to back-check previous crossword puzzles in the *Daily Telegraph*, MI5 was stunned to discover two separate puzzles in May in which were found the words UTAH and OMAHA, both codenames for landing sites on the Normandy coast. Three days after their initial discovery, on May 31, just seven days before the invasion, the word MULBERRY was the answer to the clue, "This bush is a center of nursery revolutions." MULBERRY was the codename for the floating harbors that were to be towed across the English Channel. And finally, two days later, a puzzle clue elicited the word NEPTUNE, the codename for D-Day's naval operations. That was all MI5 needed to pay a hurried visit to the home of Leonard Sidney Dawe, for twenty years the *Telegraph*'s crossword puzzle master. The flustered Dawe protested his innocence to the incredulous investigators, who, considering the imminence of the operation and the improbability of five separate occurrences of secret words in his puzzles, were reluctant to let him go. But in due time they came to understand the whole affair as one of the most incredible coincidences in military history.

Doubters and conspiracy mongers to this day question the innocence of the affair, and it is easy to understand why: The sheer improbability of it staggers the mind. Even the appearance of one codeword in a crossword puzzle would stretch credulity. But it is the word OVERLORD that really gets the skeptics overheated. In a lifetime of word usage, they posit, how many times would one hear, or use, that word? Our answer is . . . none. Was it a secret message?

"BLESSENT MON COEUR D'UNE LANGUEUR MONOTONE"

While we may never know if secret messages were buried in the crossword puzzles, there were extraordinary secret messages passed back and forth across the Channel during the D-Day invasion of Fortress Europe. The most famous of them used the opening stanza of Paul Verlaine's famous poem "Chanson d'Automne." Here's how it worked. Thousands of freedom fighters within the French Resistance were readied to commit important acts of sabotage during the invasion of France. Each group had a specific job—to cut phone lines, blow up rail tracks, destroy gas supplies, cut power cables—undertaken only when a message, specific to their cell, was broadcast over the British Broadcasting Corporation's radio service, the BBC.

A second secret message was more general in nature but equally important. This message would alert all of France that the invasion was on. It would come in two halves. The first half would be sent several days in advance of the invasion; the second half, which was necessary to confirm the first, would come just hours before the bullets would fly. Frenchmen had to be alert.

On June 1, 1944, mixed in with diversionary gibberish broadcast each night by the BBC (along with some very real messages for the Resistance) was this opening line from the Verlaine poem: *Les sanglots longs des violons de l'automne* (The long sobs of the violins of autumn). This was the first half of the D-Day invasion alert. It meant that the landings were now near; await the confirmation message.

They wouldn't wait long. At about 10:15 P.M. on June 5, 1944, these lines were broadcast: *Blessent mon coeur d'une langueur monotone* (Wound my heart with a monotonous languor).

The invasion was on.

Eight hours later the most ferocious battle in World War II history would begin on the Normandy beaches of France. The invasion of Europe was under way. What, though, of the words in the title to this chapter? This is one of hundreds, if not thousands of secret messages sent to the Resistance by the BBC, activating their cells during the D-Day invasion and specifying what target or type of sabotage to undertake. One message was "The dice are on the table," which meant cut the phone lines. Another was, "It is hot in Suez," meaning it was time to sabotage the railroad tracks.

There were thousands if not tens of thousands of secret messages flashed across the Channel during World War II, but the words of a nineteenth-century poet would go down as one of the most dramatic of them all, for it did nothing less than mark the beginning of the liberation of Europe.

THE JOKE BOMBED

The German V-1 rocket, known as a buzz bomb during the latter stages of World War II, was not an effective tactical weapon: It had no reliable guidance system by which to hit a planned target. But it was an effective terrorist weapon. It flew at low levels, giving frightened Britons both a close-up view of its menacing wings and an earful of its powerful motor. When the motor stopped running and it started falling, death was imminent.

Imagine the surprise and relief when, in January 1945, a buzz bomb streaked over the south of England and, instead of exploding, ingeniously opened and scattered crossword puzzles all over the landscape. Upon inspection, the puzzle was quickly understood to be a not-so-clever bit of propaganda, a secret message if you will, courtesy of the German High Command. Its effect was mostly comical.

But many people at the time missed its most ingenious element. It would have been worth an extra laugh. The arrangement of the black squares in the crossword grid spelled "V-1."

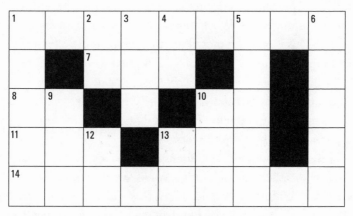

PUZZLE No. 30
The V-1 Puzzle

ACROSS

1. He is your enemy, too.
7. V-1 is so fast, that it is hard to this.
8. Partly a beverage.
10. This is the beginning of a German victory.
11. We hear that this is a rare commodity in England.
13. This is Latin.
14. He wants all you've got.

DOWN

1. In the case of the air war, he has been bit by V-1.
2. Money, but no pence.
3. Men and material intended for Normandy very often finish up at the bottom of this.
4. V-1 contains this.
5. Britain has none at inter-Allied conferences.
6. At Teheran, Churchill practically did this before Stalin.
9. First person singular.
10. Two reprisals with nothing in between.
12. Warmongers must this, if England is to be saved.
13. That man.

11:

DOG LEG LEFT

SECRET MESSAGING has typically flourished in the most stressful of situations—the D-Day invasion codes, the Navajo code talkers in the South Pacific, the quilts of the Underground Railroad, to name just a few. Little wonder, then, that some of the most unusual stories of secret messaging come out of perhaps the most troubling of all situations—the war in Vietnam.

BAT 21

As he parachuted slowly toward the ground, Lieutenant Colonel Iceal Hambleton could only watch as his EB-66 "Tiny Tim" radar jamming aircraft (callsign BAT 21) plunged into the jungle, afire and coming apart. His buddies were all dead. A North Vietnamese SA-2 "Guideline" missile had hit the plane, and only Hambleton, the navigator, had been able to jump away from the flaming fuselage.

It was 1972. The Vietnam War was winding down, but Hambleton had volunteered for this mission, leading a stream of B-52s to bombing locations south of the DMZ. Now the whole thing had gone sour. The steaming Vietnamese jungle was down below him, and rushing up fast.

As he hit the ground, the real nightmare began. A forward air controller had seen him float into a jungle canopy, and he knew where he was. Night was coming soon, but a "snatch" rescue might be possible. An Army "Huey," callsign Blueghost 39, made the attempt. It was shot to pieces. Three men were killed and a fourth was captured.

Over the next eleven days, in the most involved search-and-rescue operation of the Vietnam War, Colonel Hambleton eluded enemy forces numbering some thirty thousand men, and also directed bombing support on his own position, and did it without benefit of food and with very little water. The only resources Hambleton had at his disposal were a hand-held radio and a team of low-flying observers who were his eyes in the sky, keeping him apprised of enemy movements and positions. While Hambleton was trying to stay alive on the ground, the helicopter rescue attempts were all failures. In addition to the Huey, five more aircraft were shot down, eight more men were killed, two were captured, and two more parachuted into the jungle as Hambleton had done. Suddenly there were three aviators to rescue.

The job fell to the Special Forces' Joint Personnel Rescue Center, led by Lieutenant Colonel Andy Anderson. Anderson organized a land rescue, realizing that only a small, stealthy party could infiltrate an area in which there were so many enemy troops. But to do that, the three aviators had to be directed away from the enemy to quieter, more out-of-the-way locations. This could be done, since all three men had survival radios. But the enemy was eavesdropping on the radio frequency, hoping to hear the rescue plans. So a secret message system was quickly invented for each man. For Hambleton it was easy. He was a four-handicap golfer, and had played at nearly every Air Force golf course there was, especially at Shaw, McDill, and Hickam Air Force bases. Using these layouts as "maps" that only they and Hambleton knew, the rescuers—Navy SEAL Lieutenant Tom Norris and Petty Officer Nguyen van Kiet—directed Hambleton hole by hole, asking him to walk the distance of certain golf holes with a "0" added to it. Finally he reached the "green," where Norris and Kiet were waiting. As they whisked him to safety, Hambleton asked his rescuers where they were going. Where else? "The nineteenth hole!"

Working the Wall

The unfortunate men who were incarcerated in the Vietnamese prison camps named the Hanoi Hilton, the Heartbreak Hotel, and New Guy Village were certainly shining examples of courage, devotion to duty, and toughness. They were also among the cleverest secret message senders in military history.

To get around the jailers' strict enforcement of their "no communication" policy, they used a wide variety of ingenious methods to talk and write to each other. Communication was all-important to the men, for it kept them organized and encouraged, and imparted a feeling of comradeship that was crucial to survival. They used tried-and-true methods of secret writing, such as plain-text letters written with burnt matchsticks on toilet paper. They wrote messages on food and waste pail handles. They carved letters underneath tin plates. They whistled "Yankee Doodle Dandy" greetings to new arrivals. But their crowning achievement was the creation and implementation of the "tap" code.

This was a communications system based on sound, usually communicated by tapping on cell walls with the finger or a solid object. POWs called it "working the wall." Versions of sound codes have been around for centuries, but the closest precursor of this tap code was the one used by the British in the early years of the twentieth century and taught to American POWs in World War I. An Air Force captain named Carlyle Harris is generally given credit for introducing the tap code to the Hanoi Hilton in 1965.

To generate correspondence, each POW had to first memorize a five-by-five matrix of the alphabet. It looked like this:

	1	**2**	**3**	**4**	**5**
1	A	B	C	D	E
2	F	G	H	I	J
3	L	M	N	O	P
4	Q	R	S	T	U
5	V	W	X	Y	Z

(The K is not included; Cs substitute for Ks.)

To transmit a message, one would "tap" a number equal to its letter value, using the first tap to indicate the horizontal number, and the second tap for the vertical number. For example, two taps followed by two taps would indicate the letter G. The most common message sent back and forth, in fact, was 2-2, 2-1, 4-5 (G-B-Y, or God Bless You).

The tap code was ideal because it was easy to learn, and versatile when it had to be. One could "tap" in other ways than just finger tapping. Coughs or sweeps of a broom could do just as well. New prisoners were taught the matrix within hours of their arrival. They found it stuffed into their prison uniform pockets while they were in the bath area, or under a rock in the latrine. One POW, after being knocked to the floor by a guard in the torture room, looked up and spotted the matrix carved into the underside of a table with the words, "All prisoners learn this code!"

Abbreviation was necessary with the code. Most POWs became very adept at shortening words, as this message demonstrates:

GM LGU Z IZ IN PS ALRDY HIT F BIO X 5 NOW GETG THRTS F BIO X PB
LTR FM HOME X LL FOX IS NEW XO X NEW NAME LCDR RENDER CRAY-
TON NO OTH INFO X PB N BP Q W SPOT SOS

(Good morning. Larry Guardino says twelve men in the Pigsty have already been tortured for biographies. Five men are now being threatened with torture if they do not write biographies. Phil Butler got letter from home. Looks like Fox is the new executive officer of the camp. A new validated prisoner name is Lieutenant Commander Render Crayton. We have no further information on him. Phil Butler and Bob Peel had quizzes with Spot—same old shit.)

Perhaps the most famous messaging occurred after the North Vietnamese played an antiwar message from an American folksinger over the camp loudspeaker. Within minutes the message had gotten all the way around camp: 5-2, 4-3, 1-1, 3-3, 2-1, 1-1, 5-1, 5-5, 3-4, 5-4, 3-1, 3-1, 3-4 (Joan Baez Succs).

12:

BUSY SIGNALS FOR BUSY PEOPLE

PEOPLE WHO WORK IN UNIQUE JOBS for a long period of time often develop a language so particularly specialized that it becomes a kind of secret code in and of itself. To an outsider listening in, the words they use have no meaning. How do these codes begin in the first place? Quite likely, they were a function of speed or efficiency. Why use a three-word phrase such as "random-access memory" when the acronym "RAM" will do, and it sounds good, too? With use, the acronym becomes the norm, then it itself may be abbreviated, or changed into a verb or adjective, and voilà—a word strays into the secret language of jargon, where it can be used to send and receive provocative coded messages.

WHAT'LL YA HAVE . . . THE VARSITY

Located in Atlanta, Georgia, hard by the campus of Georgia Tech, The Varsity is known as the World's Largest Drive-In Restaurant, selling more Coca-Cola than any other single restaurant in the world. From its famous 150-foot-long stainless-steel counter come hot dogs, chili dogs, hamburgers, chili burgers, onion rings, and french fries in sufficient quantities to feed the thousands of people who flock in every day. It is also the birthplace of the most original short-order language in the country. Ever since its humble beginnings in 1928, The Varsity has been a busy place, and there is a premium placed on getting your order in quickly. Two miles of hot dogs, a ton of onions, twenty-five hundred pounds of potatoes, and five thousand fried pies are served every day. To do that the red-coated servers have invented a secret short-order lingo that always starts with, "What'll ya have?" (And you better be ready. One of The Varsity's mottoes is, "Have your mind on your order and your order on your mind.")

You want a hot dog to go with onions on the side, potato chips, and a chocolate milk? The sing-song order is heard above the crowd noise: "Walk a dog sideways, bag of rags and N.I.P.C. Next!"

If you're a first-timer, you won't know what was just said. But over time everyone learns the language. If you know it, you can use it and the staff will appreciate it. It speeds things along and makes their jobs much easier. Here's the starter lexicon:

HOT DOG: A hot dog with chili and mustard.
HEAVY WEIGHT: Same as hot dog but with extra chili.
NAKED DOG: A plain hot dog in a bun.
MK DOG: A hot dog with mustard and ketchup.
REGULAR C DOG: A hot dog with chili, mustard, and ketchup.
RED DOG: Hot dog with ketchup only.
YELLOW DOG: Hot dog with mustard only.
YANKEE DOG: Same as a yellow dog.
WALK A DOG (OR STEAK): A hot dog to go.
STEAK: A hamburger with mustard, ketchup, and pickle.
CHILI STEAK: A hamburger with Varsity chili.
GLORIFIED STEAK: A hamburger with mayonnaise, lettuce, and tomato.
MARY BROWN STEAK: A plain hamburger with no bun (can also enjoy the hot dog version).
NAKED STEAK: A plain steak (can also be called a Sally Rand steak).
VARSITY ORANGE: The original formula.
N.I. ORANGE: No ice orange.

F.O.: Frosted orange.

JOE-REE: Coffee with cream.

P.C.: Plain chocolate milk (always served with ice).

N.I.P.C.: No ice, plain chocolate milk.

ALL THE WAY: With onions; can be hot dog, chili steak, etc.

BAG OF RAGS: Potato chips.

RING ONE: Order of onion rings.

STRINGS: French fries.

SIDEWAYS: Onions on the side.

THE HARVEY GIRLS AND THE CUP AND SAUCER CODE

It is said that no one did more to tame the wild American West than Fred Harvey, whose Harvey Houses provided food and shelter to the thousands of men and women who headed west on the Santa Fe Railroad in the 1880s.

To staff the numerous Harvey restaurants springing up along the rail routes, Harvey used newspaper ads to recruit thousands of unmarried women as employees, many of them newly arrived immigrants. The work required good manners, a neat, clean appearance, a sharp black-and-white uniform, and a willingness to work from morning until night. In return, they earned thirty dollars per month, free room and board, and had an annual free ticket to travel anywhere on the Santa Fe line. One hundred thousand women from 1883 to 1959 became "Harvey Girls," making Fred Harvey the largest single employer in the West.

A Harvey Girl's workday centered on the arrival and departure of the trains, the short layovers the rail companies allowed for travelers to stretch their legs and grab a bite to eat. Short, however, was the key word. Trains had schedules and the stops were precisely timed. The Harvey Houses, however, were trained and ready. A telegraph would let them know how many people would be on each train, and how many to expect for dinner. The tables were laid, the doors open, a barker on the steps of the depot—and the girls were standing at the door of their restaurant.

The key to the operation was speed: The Harvey Girls knew that they had to feed hundreds of passengers in thirty minutes or less so the train could stay on schedule. With that efficiency in mind, there were no menus—the meal was the same for everybody. The only variable was one's drink choice—coffee, tea, milk, or iced tea—which, at first, presented a time problem for the Girls, at least until they invented a clever code technique to speed up the process. As the waitress went from table to table, she took the beverage orders then adjusted the position of the cup and saucer in front of each patron. As the servers came behind her, they needed to do no more than look at the position of the cups and glasses on the table to know which drink to pour. Cup face up, in the saucer—that's coffee!

13:

WHEN VOICES WON'T WORK

IT LOOKED LIKE CHAOS. Hundreds of men and women were hustling and bustling about, bumping into each other, standing on their toes, waving their arms, their hands clutching slips of paper or clipboards or a pen. Voices rose on top of each other, arms shot into the air frantically gesturing for attention, each person trying harder to be heard than the next.

It was a place aptly named "the pit."

A thousand miles away, in the utter calm of a quiet river, on a cold Colorado morning, two kayakers slipped though the waters three hundred meters apart, their thin boats leaving only a faint ripple to mark their passage. The lead kayaker looked back, and when he did, he dipped the blade of his paddle into the water and drew a stroke in reverse. Behind him, his partner was holding his hand high in the air with all five fingers clasped in an angry fist.

He pulled over.

What could two kayakers on a quiet river have in common with hundreds of men and women in a place called the pit?

The secret communication of hand signals.

Hand signals are a marvelous medium of secret messaging, and not only of secret messagers, either. Hand signaling is a way for people to communicate when the environment is too loud to allow them to be heard or the distances too great to span, or the voice floating on the wind too dangerous. Indeed, even with human lives and millions of dollars at stake, hand signaling is often the most efficient, effective, and accurate medium yet for messaging.

Where do we find hand signals? In settings as diverse as scuba diving, kayaking, and mountaineering; on construction sites, at airports, and on aircraft carriers; at the mercantile exchanges, with the Boy Scouts and Cub Scouts, and, of course, in the military, and not in just the obvious ways.

THE LOOKOUT

In the movie *Saving Private Ryan* a soldier climbs up into a bell tower to be the squad's lookout. Forty feet off the ground, he has an impressive view of the approaches to their position and, equally, can see his captain (Tom Hanks) on the ground. But he's too high to communicate by voice without risk of detection. In one scene, Hanks looks up to his lookout, who starts to send back a message. He spreads two fingers and points to his eyes, then extends his hand out, palm down, and wiggles it in an undulating motion. He follows this gesture by holding up three fingers. Hanks's character reads the message. "I see thirty men on foot coming directly toward us."

The military is an avid user of hand signals, and for good reason. In the scene from *Saving Private Ryan*, with the noise of men setting up machine-gun nests, pushing aside piles of broken bricks, loading ammo, and stringing wire through the debris, who knows how many words might be garbled. Worse, what wasn't heard on the ground might carry on the wind and be heard by the enemy. The lookout used well-known military hand signals to communicate with precision, quickly, all the while maintaining silence, a precious military asset.

Sealed in the Cockpit

Hand signals are also used to bring order to the chaos on an aircraft carrier flight deck. Sealed inside the cockpit, the radio in his headphones tuned to the tower frequency, a Navy pilot is almost completely cut off from the environment around him. Deck handlers in colored shirts swarm around his jet but the roar of his engines, the hiss of the catapult steam, and the blowing of a twenty-knot wind make words insignificant. Hand signals are the only hope.

As the pilot sits in the quiet of his cockpit, his eyes sweep the carrier deck for the only person who communicates with him—the yellow-shirted plane director. Let's say the yellow shirt raises both arms and clenches his fists. If he then crosses his arms at his wrists, he is telling the pilot to apply both brakes and bring the jet to a full stop. If he kneels and taps one finger on the flight deck, he is telling the pilot, and everyone around the aircraft, that the launch is a go. Whoosh! The F/A-18 Hornet streaks down the catapult and rockets into the sky.

The pilot has a very important hand signal that he's expected to use, too. When he sees the boys in the red jerseys coming toward his aircraft he places his hands on a bar next to the canopy bow, or in a place that is equally conspicuous. The red shirts look up, see his hands, nod, and scurry under the jet. What's going on? The red shirts are the weaponeers. They're about to go under the jet and secure the missiles. Before they do, they make sure that the pilot's hands aren't on anything, so that he can't press the wrong button and fire a rocket into their faces or start to taxi the plane and crush them. So the pilot puts his hands up, in clear view, to show them that he won't touch a thing.

All communicated without using precious radio time.

Hand signals let messagers communicate across some unusual barriers. Consider a recording studio, the most soundproof of all environments. A thick glass wall separates the artist, who might be plinking a guitar riff or laying down a vocal track, from the producer. They can see each other, of course, but they can't hear each other. If they do want to talk, the producer will beckon through the glass, or use the intercom, or, if the producer is fidgety and is pacing and the intercom button is too far away, they might just use hand signals. Such as: The producer points to one of the singers and then taps the top of his head. What is he saying? He's saying, "top it," or, lay down the same vocals again, one on top of the other. Topping a track adds warmth, body, and texture to a sound. In effect, the singer is accompanying himself, building the sound, one of the many tricks of professional studio producers.

Tapping the top of your head may mean to "top it" in a recording studio but not on a construction site. When you tap your fist on your head on a construction site, it means that you are sending a signal to the heavy crane operator, and no one else. Let's say you follow that gesture with another, with both fists in front of your body, thumbs out. What's going on? You're telling the operator to extend the boom.

Does that seem like a familiar gesture to you? It might be. It's the same hand signal used at airports. When the ground handlers bump their fists together with both thumbs out, they are telling the pilot of the airliner that they're pulling the chocks away from the wheels. Without those chocks, the airplane can move, so you'd better let the people in the cockpit know. Thumbs out, tap your fist together: Chocks are being pulled.

THE KAYAKER'S FIST

Sea kayakers use hand signals to communicate across the open waters where their voices might be lost to the wind, just as scuba divers use them underwater. In the beginning of this chapter, we used the example of a kayaker with a raised fist. That signal simply means, "Let's pull over." But do you know what it means when you extend one hand out, palm down, fingers curled in an angry catlike claw and then slash another finger across your throat? It says, "I didn't like what I saw in there; its too dangerous for us." That's a useful signal if you're underwater and thinking about entering an old sunken ship and there's a nest of electric eels hanging over the doorway.

Chaos in the Pit

And what about the chaos in the pit? The Chicago Mercantile Exchange runs the commodities pits. Each commodity has its own trading area or "pit." Contracts for future deliveries of soybeans and wheat and heating oil and hundreds of other commodities are bought and sold at a furious pace in the pits. Timing, of course, is everything. In commodities trading, small price increments can make or break a trader (or drive up the price of an order of french fries at McDonald's; cooking oils are sold in the pits, too).

Fearing that technology would give one trader an unfair advantage over the other, the CME doesn't allow electronic communication gear in the pits. Instead, they allow hand signals. Hand signals beautifully communicate above the din, but they have an added advantage—they help mask the identity of the buyer or seller. Because of hand signals, the trader doesn't need to carry papers into the pit or leave behind documents that might otherwise identify who's trying to corner what markets. Hand signals allow traders to secretly fill a customer's orders without identifying who the buyer or seller might be, always the subject of after-hours commodities intrigue.

So sophisticated is the CME's system of hand signals that it is possible to accurately use them to communicate buying, selling, shorting, price changes, and delivery dates in months and years—in fact, for the entire trade. Here are some examples:

> HAND UP, PALM FACING YOURSELF: I want to buy.
> PALM FACING YOU, FOUR FINGERS: I want to bid this price (ending in a 4).
> FIST TOUCHES FOREHEAD, FACING YOU: One hundred (units) of (a commodity).
> HOLDS JACKET FLAP WITH RIGHT HAND: Contracts expiring in May.
> THUMBS UP: Your order has been filled.
> FINGER TWIRLING NEXT TO FACE: Your order is still working.

14:

I RAISE A MILLION

HUMAN BEINGS have the capacity to be very expressive in nonverbal ways. A raised eyebrow can speak volumes. A shoulder shrug may tell you all you need to know. A wink supplies the necessary confirmation between conspirators. The arms, the hands, and the fingers are especially adroit at communicating with incredible nuance, as can be seen in the many sign languages available to the deaf.

The "signifying" of hand/arm/finger movements and other body gestures has always been the province of secret messages. Gesture codes are always present in matters of war, love, and money, as you'll find in these stories of auctions, baseball, war, and television.

SECRET MESSAGES AT THE AUCTION

To participate at the Saturday morning all-comers auction down at the neighborhood thrift shop, you only have to have some cash in your pocket and a hand you can raise in the air. But in the more stately environs of a high-stakes auction presided over by Sotheby's or Christie's, the preeminent houses in the auction business, the game is played very differently. There, the rules of play include the right to bid by means of secret signals, prearranged with the auction house, which allow anonymity and the ability to conceal the location and source of a bid.

Why would a bidder want to disguise the fact that he is bidding? Let's say a respected art expert enters a quiet bid on a somewhat neglected painting at auction. Other art buyers, who would certainly notice his bid, frantically check the catalogue and start bidding on the piece themselves, figuring that the expert has spotted something valuable and is trying to steal it at a low price. The expert then finds himself in a competitive situation that he was trying to avoid. If he had worked out a secret signal with the auctioneer so that the room did not know he was bidding, he probably could have walked away with the painting at a low price while no one was looking.

Whatever the reason, some auction buyers go to elaborate lengths to work out their signal systems with the auctioneer. It is a competent auctioneer, indeed, who can remember all the signals from all the players, and can spy them in the midst of a fast-moving bid sequence. Some bidders use arm or leg codes (crossed arms or legs mean a bid) or eyeglasses positions (on means a bid, off is no bid) or opening or closing the catalogue. Horse owner and trainer D. Wayne Lukas (who has since changed his signal) reveals that for years his signal to the auctioneer at the Keeneland Select Yearling Sale was to cross his legs so that his shoe stuck out in the aisle. When the auctioneer saw the shoe, he knew that Lukas was an active bidder.

CONNIE MACK, CODE MASTER

In baseball's bygone days, relief pitchers used to warm up along the first- and third-base lines, within shouting distance of the dugouts. As small baseball parks became huge stadiums, the bullpens moved deep into the outfield corners, out of reach of the manager's vocal cords. To communicate with the relievers way out there, telephones were installed.

Connie Mack, legendary manager and stickler for the old ways, never used the phone. When he was manager of the Philadelphia Athletics he worked out a secret message system with his pitchers that used only his gift for rhyming words. For example, if he wanted Bobby Shantz to warm up, he would point to his pants. And if he came out of the dugout and pointed to the stands, who did he want? Why, Carl Scheib, of course. The Athletics played their home games in Shibe Park!

BASEBALL CODES

Today, the baseball field is a cacophony of hand signals screaming back and forth from one side of the ballpark to the other. Baseball is a very tactical game, and decisions for every player—offense and defense—are made on every pitch. Consider the lines of communication. From dugout to the third-base coach. From the third-base coach to the first-base coach. From the catcher to the pitcher. To runners and infielders. Managers and coaches stroke their hats, rub their tummies, pat their arms, and touch their knees as they run through the kind of signals most kids learn in Little League.

But the signals and signs are often so complex that even professionals lose track. When the Dodgers and Oakland A's played in the 1974 World Series, Bert Campaneris came to bat with a runner on first and nobody out. Everybody on both teams knew that the third-base coach was going to signal Campaneris to bunt and move the runner to second base. He flashed the sign; Campaneris stepped out of the box, which meant, "Show me the sign again." The third-base coach gave him the sign. Again Campaneris looked confused. Andy Messersmith, who was pitching for the Dodgers, couldn't believe what he was seeing. And he was getting peeved, having to stand out on the mound while Campaneris walked around in confusion. So he yelled to the batter, "Campy, he wants you to bunt!" Campaneris understood, stepped in, and bunted the runner to second base.

Home run champ Frank Howard was a great hitter, but awful at getting signs. While playing for the Dodgers, Howard was given a simplified signal system by third-base coach Preston Gomez. For example, when they wanted him to run on the pitch, the base coach would simply call him by his last name. It seemed like a good plan, but Howard forgot. In one game, as he took his lead off first base, Pete Reisert, the first-base coach, yelled, "Atta boy, Howard," signaling him to run on the pitch. The pitcher delivered; Howard did not run. Again the coach yelled, "Stay alive, Howard!" Howard called time out and walked over to his coach. "We've been friends a long time," he said to Reisert, "and I've always called you Pete. Why have you stopped calling me Frank?"

Players, managers, and coaches aren't the only ones at the ballpark who use hand signals. The umpires have signals of their own, to indicate ball or strike, out or safe, fair or foul. These are given with exaggerated gestures that everyone can see. But it wasn't always that way. It started, they say, back in the late nineteenth century, when the umpires started using big gestures as a way to help a deaf outfielder—William "Dummy" Hoy—know how many outs there were.

But umpires have another secret signaling system, used to communicate just among themselves. For example, if you see a home-plate ump hold both hands to his side and twirl the index fingers of each, he's sending a message to the first- and third-base umps to tell them he'll cover one of the bases if the play pulls them away from their normal positions. Why the twirling fingers? Because the umps are going to rotate clockwise or counterclockwise.

Most people know that a tap of the wrist means the play is a "timed" play, which means that sometime between the second and third outs, a player can score and the run will count, but did you also know that there is no standard hand signal for an out or for a strike? An out used to be called by jerking a closed fist with a raised thumb into the air. But that seemed too old-fashioned to modern umps, so in the 1990s they got together and agreed to call outs with a plain closed fist. Not that it appears in any handbook, as such things often do in football or baseball. It doesn't.

The most problematic call of them all is the check-swing strike. A home-plate umpire often needs help from the first- or third-base umps to determine whether the batter checked his swing soon enough to avoid a strike. If the home-plate umpire pivots quickly and points firmly at one of his fellow umps, he's asking for a second opinion and he waits for the other ump's call, which will be final. This gesture, however, has been known to be laced with a few tricks. If an ump pivots and makes the gesture with his right hand, he really does want an opinion. But if he pivots and points with his left hand he's saying, "I got the call right; don't disagree, we're just making a show of this."

15 :

THE MESSAGE IS THE MEDIUM

THE WORLD OF MAGIC is a world of secrets. For thousands of years there have been performers, entertainers, and scoundrels who have used a wide variety of ingenious deceptions to amaze us, to entertain us, and occasionally, to flimflam us. One area of magic is especially reliant on the skillful use of codes and secret messages — "mentalism," also known as telepathy or mind reading. These performers are the aristocrats of magic because their intellectual and mnemonic skills are prodigious. Unlike David Copperfield, whose stage is crowded with apparatuses and big effects, mentalists stand alone on stage with only their brains and skills available to amaze the audience.

THE ESP MESSAGE

Despite numerous attempts and occasional compelling evidence, no two people in history have been able to demonstrate to science's satisfaction the ability to communicate telepathically. It's a pity, because such communication, if it could be established on a consistent basis, would constitute the ultimate secret message system. Both the CIA and the KGB have dabbled with this tantalizing possibility for years, without much luck (we understand).

But back at the turn of the twentieth century, two Englishmen named Douglas Blackburn and G. A. Smith, by means of their amazing psychic demonstrations, had the scientific establishment convinced that, for the first time in history, telepathic communication was proved to be possible.

With members of a trusted scientific society present, Smith would be blindfolded, seated in a chair, and completely covered with a dark blanket. Several paces away, Blackburn would be shown a drawing on a chalkboard, silently held by one of the society members. Blackburn, concentrating on the image and saying nothing, would hold his temples as if to "send" the message to his partner. In a few moments, Smith would say, "I have it," and would produce from under the blanket an exact reproduction of the drawing. This astounded the august company to such an extent that they had to admit the possibility of human telepathy. And if that was possible, they figured, what about all the other sorts of psychic phenomena?

Many years later they were embarrassed to learn that the whole thing had been a hoax. Blackburn himself let the cat out of the bag. They had done it, he said, "to show how easily men of scientific mind and training could be deceived."

The message, he explained, was not sent telepathically, but by standard magician's tricks. As Blackburn viewed the image on the chalkboard, he drew it surreptitiously, by means of a fingertip lead, on a cigarette paper he hid in his right palm. By prearrangement—kicking the edge of the carpet—he would signal to Smith that he had completed the drawing. Smith would then announce, "I have it!" and would reach out from under the blanket, fumbling to grasp a pen on the table. Blackburn would hand Smith his own pen, which, of course, contained the cigarette paper folded into the barrel. Hidden by the blanket, Smith merely had to lift his blindfold, see the drawing by means of a small dab of luminous paint he hid in his pocket, and draw the image on his own slate.

When executed by two professionals, with the proper amount of misdirection and timing, the effect must have been truly convincing, even to a group of skeptics. But that's what magic is all about, isn't it?

THE "MIND READERS"

Before Kreskin and other solo mentalism acts, mind reading was a two-person show, usually performed by a husband-and-wife team. One person was called the Performer or Assistant, the other was the Medium or Mentalist. The key to their act was an extraordinarily complex system of covert communications and codes. In fact, in the magic business this is called a "code act." These acts always garner the highest respect in the business. Everyone knows that the standards of quality and proficiency needed to make the act work are extraordinarily high — higher, indeed, than the code proficiency of any espionage agent in the world. Why? Because stage performers have to do three things an agent would never have to do: First, be 100 percent undetectable. If the audience can see the code in play, even slightly, it's not a successful act. Second, be fast. The sending and receiving of coded messages have to occur within seconds of each other. No agent behind enemy lines ever had to work that fast. Third, the system has to be so versatile and comprehensive that any word or any number can be sent and received. There aren't many codes that have ever been able to do that.

Let's imagine, then, a theater full of people. On stage is a man in a tuxedo. He wears a blindfold over his eyes. Out in the audience with a microphone is his assistant, a woman, who strolls up and down the theater aisles. She stops and asks a man to stand. They both face the stage, and she addresses the man on stage: "Please tell me this man's age, would you?"

The mentalist thinks a moment, then says, "That handsome gentleman is sixty-five years old."

The man shakes his head, amazed, "That's right! I'm sixty-five!"

As the man sits down the assistant says to the stage, "Try to tell me the number of people in the row I'm standing by."

The mentalist answers, "Easy. Twenty-one." The crowd does a quick count. He's right!

Then she asks a nearby woman for her driver's license. As she looks at it, she asks the mentalist, "Will you quickly tell me the day and date this woman's driver's license was issued, please?"

The audience murmurs in anticipation—how could he possibly know that? After a few seconds of deliberation, the mentalist says, "Ah, I have it now . . . Wednesday, July 6." The woman from whom the driver's license was borrowed peers at the numbers. She says into the microphone, a bit stunned, "That's correct." The crowd bursts into applause.

What seems impossible has just occurred, to great entertainment effect. But in fact, the mentalist has merely received a coded message from his assistant, decoded it in seconds, and orated the answer with a flourish. How did he do it?

The system (and all performers work on subtle variations of it) is based on a number/phrase code. The basic phrases are those that are normally used in everyday interrogatives:

I	means	1
TRY or GO	means	2
CAN	means	3
WILL	means	4
WOULD	means	5
PLEASE	means	6
QUICKLY	means	7
NOW	means	8
NOW THEN	means	9
SEE	means	0 or 10
NEXT	means	repeat the previous number

So, in the first question above (the man's age), the assistant gave her partner the answer with "please" and "would"—6-5. In the second she gave him "try" and "I'm"—2-1. In the third, she went to an extension of the number code for days of the week and months of the year, which looks like this:

SUNDAY	is	1
MONDAY	is	2
TUESDAY	is	3
WEDNESDAY	is	4
THURSDAY	is	5
FRIDAY	is	6
SATURDAY	is	7

Months are the same—January is 1, February is 2, and so forth.

So, for the driver's license, the assistant signaled her partner with "will" (4 is Wednesday); "quickly" (7 is July); and "please" (6). And did it in normal, everyday speech that left the crowd clueless about how the trick was performed.

The basic method of secretly signaling numbers from 1 to 10 provides the basis for not just numbers, days of the week, and months, but also virtually anything that can be listed:

- COINS: Pennies are 1s, nickels are 2s, dimes are 3s, and so on. This is how a mentalist can tell you how much change you have in your pocket, and can even give you their mint years, if somebody asks.

- COLORS: Red is 1, white is 2, blue is 3, black is 4, brown is 5, green is 6, and so on. "I'd like to know the color of this lady's hat." Answer: "Red." (I equals 1 equals red.) "And what color is her hat, please?" Answer: "Green." (Please equals 6 equals green.)

To execute the codes as described above, the performers obviously have to memorize the various codes, and practice, practice, practice. Not an easy thing to do, but not nearly as difficult as the alphabet code, which is a further extension of the system. Using the alphabet code, the performers can communicate virtually any letters, words, or numbers in the English language. The code is still based on the basic number code, and is constructed like this:

1 = a = I
2 = b = TRY or GO
3 = c = CAN
4 = d = WILL

and so on, through the double-digit numbers, which get more complicated, ending with:

26 = z = TRY/GO/PLEASE

So, with the system in place, the assistant can ask such questions as, "I am thinking of two letters now. Try and tell me what they are, can you?" Which is code for 18/23, or the letters R and W.

To make it even more complex, some performers even go to the trouble of matching hundreds of everyday objects (the kind people would have in their pockets) with the wording of a question, so that when the assistant says, "I want you to tell me what I hold in my hand," the mentalist can say, "A watch." If she had said, "What do I hold in my hand?" he would say, "A diamond ring."

What other lists could they match up? Countries, cities, playing cards, first names, last names, brand names, shoe styles—virtually anything. An experienced mind-reading team, using their full powers of memory, cannot be stumped by anything . . . and that is the desired effect. Clairvoyance!

There are dozens of other mentalist methods for two people, involving miniature radio transmitters, blinking lights, sounds, twitching of jacket sleeves, and so on, but only one other is held in high esteem among performers, and that is a time code. Talk about difficult! Here's the scene:

The mentalist and his assistant sit on opposite ends of a long table. A number is written on a piece of paper. It is shown to the audience—

a 7. It is handed to the assistant, who reads it, then hands it back. The assistant and the mentalist then stare at each other. No words are spoken, no arms, legs, or heads move. After a few excruciatingly silent moments, the mentalist takes pen in hand and writes down a number. Of course, it is a 7. How does he do it? By means of a precisely timed counting method, worked out over many months of practice with the assistant.

After the number is seen by the assistant, she raises her eyes to meet those of her partner. As soon as she blinks once, the count begins: ONE Mississippi, TWO Mississippi, THREE Mississippi, up to the target number, whereupon the assistant blinks again. The mentalist stops counting when he sees the second blink. The key, of course, is regulating the pace of the count so both people count together, and that takes practice. As always, the target number can stand for a number, or an object, or a city, or anything else worked out in advance of the trick.

THE HOUDINI MESSAGE

Harry Houdini is remembered today as the first, and perhaps best, escape artist who ever lived. But the amazing escapes were just one facet of his long professional life in the magic business. Houdini studied and perfected all variations of the prestidigitation game, from small sleight-of-hand tricks to the big, theater-sized gimmicks.

He was a showman and loved the entertainment effect of a good act, but he always stayed on the rational, logical side of things. His interest was in the science of how tricks worked, not in the mumbo-jumbo. That's why the spiritualism craze of the 1920s offended him so much. So-called "spirit mediums" were making good money holding séances all over the United States, duping thousands of people into believing that the dead were speaking to them and manifesting themselves in one way or another. Houdini had seen all the tricks before, considered them cheap, and went on a debunking crusade to show the public exactly how they were done.

The irony is that Houdini wanted to believe that communication with the dead was possible. After his beloved mother died, Houdini experimented with various means of communicating with her, all to no avail. But he always said that if there was a way to communicate between death and life, he would find it. He was a consummate planner, and he and his wife, Bess, worked out a ten-word secret message between them, which Houdini said he would communicate to her, if it was possible, after his death.

In 1926, on his deathbed, Houdini reminded Bess of the message. He died on October 31 — Halloween. For years after, Bess spent every Sunday, at the hour of his death, in her room with a photograph of Houdini, waiting for a sign. She received none. She also offered a ten-thousand-dollar reward to any spirit medium who could reveal Houdini's secret message. For two years no one could, until Arthur Ford came along.

Arthur Ford called himself the "pastor" of the First Spiritualist Church in New York. In the fall of 1928 he loudly claimed to have contacted Houdini, and said he could reveal the secret message Houdini promised to communicate from the grave. At a séance attended by five people, including an editor of *Scientific American*, Ford produced these ten words: "Rosabelle," "answer," "tell," "pray," "answer," "look," "tell," "answer," "answer," "tell." The words were duly written down and taken to Bess, who was reported to have said, "It is right." After a pause, she asked, "Did he say 'Rosabelle'? My God!" Rosabelle had been Houdini's pet name for her.

So the message was revealed . . . but what did it mean? After the name Rosabelle, the message made no sense. Two nights later, a final séance was held, with Bess in attendance. Ford, from his trance, said that Houdini explained that the words were a code — one that Bess would recognize. And she remembered. In the early days of their marriage, they had performed a mentalism act in which certain phrases were code words for numbers, colors, or letters of the alphabet. Using the code, Bess put the puzzle together. The words, in sequence, stood for the letters B-E-L-I-E-V-E. Houdini's secret message was therefore, "Rosabelle, believe!"

It makes a sensational story, but it doesn't end there. Two days after covering the final séance and splashing the results across the front page, a New York tabloid called the *Graphic* ran this even more sensational headline: "HOUDINI HOAX EXPOSED!" A reporter named Rea Jaure, who had been involved with Bess on a Houdini biography, but who was furious when Bess canceled the project, wrote that Bess and Arthur Ford had planned the whole thing as a prelude to the theatrical tour they were planning! Ford, she said, was fronting the money for the tour; Bess just had to supply the secret code, and thereby give the act a million dollars worth of publicity.

Bess, for her part, denied it. Ford also stuck to his story. But the tour was off, soured by the accusation and the taint of fakery.

On the tenth anniversary of Houdini's death, a final séance was held, this time in Hollywood. In front of a huge crowd, and a national radio audience, Bess and her new companion, Eddy Saint, implored Houdini to reveal himself. The result was . . . silence. At this, Bess officially closed the book on the whole idea of after-death communications from her husband. She said good-bye with the most unsecret message she could muster: "Good night, Harry!"

AN ARTHURIAN LEGEND

Countless preachers have recounted the great prank Sir Arthur Conan Doyle reportedly pulled on some of his closest friends. In a mischievous mood, Doyle anonymously sent the following telegram to twelve of his friends. It said, "Flee at once, your secret is discovered." (Some versions have it as "all has been discovered.")

Within twenty-four hours, so this story goes, all twelve recipients of the mysterious message had left the country!

16:

THE MESSAGE IN THE NOTES

IT'S BEEN TRUE since Gabriel blew his horn: The sound of music is often the sound of secret messages. A cavalry bugler blasts out certain notes and a hundred horsemen form into predetermined formations. The BBC uses the first four notes of Beethoven's Fifth Symphony as its announcement of coded messages to war-torn Europe. A journalist in the late 1960s avers that Paul McCartney is dead, and the proof is hidden in the Beatles' albums. A nation of teenagers, who have heard that the words are "dirty," strain to understand the brilliantly disguised warblings of the Kingsmen in the song "Louie, Louie."

Music can be the message, can hide the message, or can announce the message, as we will see in the following four stories.

PAUL IS DEAD?

Although Paul McCartney was very much alive in the summer of 1969, there were millions of people around the world who thought he was dead. It had become more than just a rumor; it was a bona fide urban legend. The "Paul is dead" phenomenon was picked up by the press and run as if it were a news item. Among other things, conspiracy nuts alleged that McCartney had died in 1966; that he had been replaced by an impostor; that the Beatles' corporate administrators tried to hush up the death to preserve the long-term viability of the group; and that there were "clues" in the Beatles' records and album art that proved he was dead.

One of the clues went back to the album *The Beatles* (also known as *The White Album*), on which John Lennon is claimed to have whispered in the song "I'm So Tired": "Paul is dead . . . miss him." To hear it, one was told, you had to play the song at very slow speeds. Others said you had to play it backward. This millions of teenagers did on their poor turntables, which never worked the same again after their motors were burned up and their gears were stripped by forcing them to turn the wrong way.

Another musical clue was the line Lennon allegedly utters at the end of "Strawberry Fields": "I buried Paul."

A visual clue supposedly appeared on the back cover of the *Sgt. Pepper* album, where McCartney is the only Beatle to face backward, and George Harrison is said to be pointing at a clock whose face indicates the hour of Paul's death.

With this rampant rumor as a backdrop, the four Beatles prepared for a photo shoot on August 8, 1969, outside their Abbey Road studios. The photo was to be the cover of the soon-to-be released *Abbey Road* album. As all Beatle fans now know, this photograph was the most provocative and mysterious cover shot in the Beatles catalogue, and perhaps in all of rock history. For it fueled the Paul Is Dead phenomenon to unbelievable heights, even while trying to defuse it. For a worldwide audience looking for more clues, this album cover gave it to them — in spades. To this day, people swear that the number of clues in the photo can lead one to only one conclusion. But since we know McCartney is very much alive, the "evidence" can be dismissed, while at the same time we can admit that the visual clues are curious.

What are the "secret messages" in the picture?

- All four men are evenly spaced, walking in the same direction, with their left legs forward. But McCartney is out of step with the others, leading with his right.

- McCartney has on a dark suit with no shoes or socks, typical of dead bodies in open caskets.

- McCartney's eyes are closed; or, if not totally closed, then glazed over, as in death.

- Lennon, dressed in white, represents the preacher/holy man who will preside over McCartney's funeral. George, dressed in blue jeans, represents the gravedigger. Ringo, in a dark suit, represents the undertaker.

- The license plate of a Volkswagen on the street is 28IF, meaning that McCartney would have been twenty-eight if he had lived (twenty-seven actually, but who's counting?).

The phenomenon soon had to die, since McCartney was so palpably alive and in public. The affair simply proved that people have an affinity for secret messages and conspiracies, and will sometimes find them where they do not exist.

A final Beatles note: On the British version of *Sgt. Pepper*, there is a real secret message included. At the end of "A Day in the Life" (the song that ends with the "endless chord"), an eight-second twenty-thousand-Hertz tone is laid down. But you won't hear it. At twenty thousand Hertz it is above the human ear's audible range. Your dog will hear it, though. And that was the point. It was supposedly a secret message from Paul McCartney to his sheepdog, Martha, for whom he later wrote the song "Martha My Dear."

ALL THE KINGSMEN

The background music for the fall of 1963 was an irresistible rock/dance classic, "Louie, Louie," by a band called the Kingsmen. It has become perhaps the most popular rock single in history, and certainly the most infamous.

Right after its release, the song raced up the charts. American teenagers could not get enough of it. Sure, nobody could understand the lyrics, but that has never been a big problem for partying teens. It was the beat that got them, and the raw simplicity of the sound. It may have been only three chords, but they were the right three chords. But soon a rumor swept High School U.S.A. like the Mother of all Hurricanes: The lyrics to "Louie, Louie" were dirty!

Well, that did it. Whoever did not own the record went and bought the record. And played it. And played it. The truly hip and knowledgeable types soon had the supposedly risqué lyrics figured out, and in days the whole teen nation—from Los Angeles to Boston—was in on the secret, naughty message.

It wasn't long before adults got wind of this, and had a typical 1960s-style hysterical reaction. Even the FBI got in on it, launching a nearly three-year investigation that yielded a 120-page report. The Bureau's published version of the song lyrics, included in all sincerity in a 1964 investigative report, contains such lines as, "Louie, Louie, oh no, get her way down low," and other, cruder howlers.

Turns out that the song had been written seven years earlier by a Louisianan named Richard Berry, and had been recorded several times, notably by Berry himself and by Robin Roberts and the Wailers. The song is about a Jamaican sailor a long way from home who tells a bartender named Louie about a girl he misses. Suffice it to say that any lyrics that are perceived to be pornographic in the Kingsmen version result from lead singer Jack Ely's tortured pronunciation, which an entire generation remembers fondly.

A MOTHER GOOSE MYSTERY

It's a pretty scene. The first-graders hold hands in a big circle, move to the music, and sing, "Ring around the rosie, pocket full of posey." But we wonder whether any of the smiling parents know the grisly origins of that song, or the secret messages it hides?

The predominant interpretation of this rhyme is that, like all good nursery rhymes, "Ring Around the Rosie" is oral history, reflecting real events of a real era. In this case the era is the seventeenth century, and the place is London, where a plague killed thousands of people in about 1665. In the midst of this holocaust, some experts believe "Ring Around the Rosie" was written as a sort of rhyming incantation to ward off the disease. In this interpretation, each line of the rhyme has a rather grisly reference to how people dealt with the plague:

- **"RING AROUND THE ROSIE"**: The ring around the rosie is a reference to the blisters with reddish sores that formed on the skin of someone infected with the disease.

- **"POCKET FULL OF POSIES"**: The posy was a bouquet of certain flowers thought to have a preventive and curative power, and was kept in the pocket for that reason, or for cloaking the smell of rotting bodies.

- **"ASHES, ASHES"**: This line might originally have been: "A-tishoo, A-tishoo," which makes more sense, a-tishoo being the sound of sneezing, which accompanied the disease.

- **"WE ALL FALL DOWN"**: What else could this be but a reference to death?

What a gruesome origin for a song that accompanies the games of children! Perhaps so gruesome that it is just not true. Many scholars contend that the rhyme didn't appear until late in the eighteenth century, and could not be about a plague that occurred more than a century earlier. Others say that the earliest versions of the rhyme are quite different from the one that survives today, and no plague references exist in it.

It appears that one can say about "Rosie" what one can say about any nursery rhyme—that its origins are murky and buried in the distant past, but that it certainly means something more than simple whimsy. What are their secret messages?

THE TWELVE DAYS OF PERSECUTION?

Many Christians believe that the song popularly called the "Twelve Days of Christmas" is not simply a fun Christmas carol, but that it is a song based in Christian history and traces its origin back to a time when Christians were persecuted for their beliefs. The song, they believe, was a secret message of Christian affirmation in the face of government-sanctioned oppression, whose aim was to preserve and pass down the articles of faith. The "gifts" given by "my true love" (God) on each of the twelve days are symbols, they contend, for the teachings of faith.

The twelve days are the span of time known as Christmastide, extending from Christmas day (December 25) to the Feast of the Epiphany (January 6). The basics of the symbolism are as follows:

FIRST DAY:

> A *partridge in a pear tree*—Jesus Christ, who died on the cross as a gift to Man from God.

SECOND DAY:

> *Two turtle doves*—The Old and New Testaments.

THIRD DAY:

> *Three French hens*—Faith, hope, and love, the gifts of the Spirit.

FOURTH DAY:

> *Four calling birds*—The four Gospels, Matthew, Mark, Luke, and John.

FIFTH DAY:

> *Five golden rings*—The Books of Moses, the Pentateuch.

SIXTH DAY:

> *Six geese a' laying*—The six days of creation.

SEVENTH DAY:

> *Seven swans a' swimming*—Wisdom, understanding, piety, fear of God, knowledge, fortitude, judiciousness (the Seven Gifts of the Holy Spirit).

EIGHTH DAY:

Eight maids a' milking—The eight beatitudes.

NINTH DAY:

Nine ladies dancing—The nine fruits of the Holy Spirit.

TENTH DAY:

Ten lords a' leaping—The Ten Commandments.

ELEVENTH DAY:

Eleven pipers piping—The eleven faithful disciples.

TWELFTH DAY:

Twelve drummers drumming—The twelve belief statements of the Apostles' Creed.

As lovely as that interpretation may be, and as numerous as are its proponents, it must be said that many scholars dispute its facts. The song, they say, dates back a few centuries, not a few millennia. And where was the open practice of Christianity banned since, say, the mid-1600s? Answer: Nowhere in the Western Hemisphere. Perhaps the song pertains to Catholics in Tudor England, persecuted by the new Anglican Church? This makes more sense until one realizes that the elements of the Scripture the song allegedly tries to preserve (the Gospels, the Pentateuch) were not inimical to the Anglican Church. In fact, scripturally both churches had virtually the same Bible.

So where did the song come from, and is it a secret message? There are many ideas out there, but most can coalesce into one predominant idea—that the song does, indeed, have symbolic religious meaning for each of the twelve days. But the origins spring not from a surreptitious attempt to preserve Christian teachings in a hostile climate, but merely as a game to teach the Catechism.

17:

WHAT MORSE WROUGHT

T HE DEVELOPMENT and implementation of Samuel Morse's telegraphic communications system changed the world. As happens in all such paradigm shifts, whole economic, social, and financial worlds lurched and transformed. Certainly the world of espionage and clandestine messaging changed utterly, as we will see in these five Morse-related stories.

THE MORSE MESSAGE

In the 1840s, an American, Samuel F. B. Morse, was among a handful of people around the world working to develop a means of long-distance communication based on electricity. Morse's system used electromagnets to power electrical signals along a wire, in sufficient strength to cause a graphic instrument on the receiving end to make a series of dots and dashes on paper. Morse soon added a second device to the system that converted the electrical signals to sound. These dots and dashes, both on paper and aloud, were simple substitutes for the letters of the alphabet and common English punctuation. As Morse's system found favor both in the United States and Europe the system was standardized and became known as Morse Code, even though, strictly speaking, it is not a code at all.

After several fits and starts, and a cash infusion from the U.S. Congress, Morse oversaw the erection of a thirty-seven-mile-long wire landline from Washington to Baltimore. On May 24, 1844, he was ready to send his first message. Seated in the Capitol Building in Washington, Morse tapped out the following:

.-- .... . .- -   .... .- - ....   --. --- -..   .-- .-. --- ..- --. .... . -

Over in Baltimore, the dots and dashes came to life on the paper tape, which was advanced along by a clock mechanism. This first successful transmission in the history of telegraphy was decoded from a codebook by jubilant journalists at a Baltimore newspaper. The message? What hath God wrought.

FROM THE ELECTRICAL FIELD TO THE BALL FIELD

Morse Code took off so fast after its first practical use in 1844 that the largest private telegraph company, Western Union, had nearly four thousand offices only twenty years later. The original Morse Code expanded to include International Morse Code (which was slightly different) and a large catalogue of two- and three-letter abbreviations for commonly used English words and phrases, to speed up transmissions.

Even though Morse Code is no longer the world standard for radio transmissions, many of those abbreviations are still in common use today, such as HQ for "headquarters," DX for "distance," RE for "concerning," ASAP for "as soon as possible," and SOS for "save our ship," the Morse distress call.

Two numbers are in common use, too—88 means "love and kisses" and 73 means "best regards" or "good luck." The latter term was used so frequently in the 1940s and '50s that it found its way out of the Morse Code world into the mainstream world of sports, especially professional baseball. In fact, it still exists today. You've heard it before, clapped and stamped out by the feet of thousands of fans who want to start a ninth-inning rally . . . dum-dum/dum-dum-dum/dum-dum-dum/ let's go! They don't know it, but the message they are sending to the batter is International Morse Code—73—Good Luck! In code it looks like this:

dash-dash-dot-dot-dot (7), dot-dot-dot-dash-dash (3).

TAKING THE FIFTH

J. O. Kerbey was a perfect choice as a spy for the Union army. He was a trained telegraph operator; he was from Maryland, a border state whose citizens could be either Yankees or Confederates; and he was a staunch supporter of the Union cause.

Feigning loyalty to the South, he offered his services to General Nathan Beauregard and found himself attached to an ideal post—at a telegraph office. From there Kerbey could monitor and overhear all the Morse traffic to and from Richmond, the Confederate capital. One day he overheard an important bit of intelligence—a field report from Manassas describing the rebel troops as decimated by illness and dysentery. It was news Kerbey felt compelled to get to Union commander McDowell. After failing to get the message to him in person, Kerbey discovered a sympathetic courier who agreed to deliver his secret message to McDowell's headquarters in Washington. The message Kerbey sent to the general was completely innocent, discussing the weather and personal matters. But there was a message in the letter. The key to finding it lay in the scribbled marks at the top. They were the Morse characters for the numeral five and the word "word." Together they formed an instruction—to read every fifth word of the letter. Doing so revealed the real message:

"Been all through Southern Army, again obliged delay here account sickness impossible Confederate advance are exhausted half army sick balance are demoralized look under front portion Blanks house situated on hill road Manassas to Washington black roll of papers official proofs wish friend Covode secure them officers are there night students Georgetown signal South from dormitory will be home soon as I can."

The reference to the Blanks house concerns the location of a complete transcript of the medical condition of the Confederate army at Manassas, stashed under the front porch by Kerbey as he was detained by a rebel patrol. The Georgetown reference is a bonus bit of intelligence Kerbey discovered on his ramblings near Washington. Apparently Georgetown College students sympathetic to the Southern cause were flashing Morse messages at night by means of lanterns in their dormitory rooms to waiting rebel couriers.

The USS *SQUALUS*

Two hundred thirty-two feet beneath the surface of the Atlantic Ocean lay the submarine USS *Squalus*. It was May 23, 1939. At first light, the *Squalus* had departed the cove at the mouth of the Piscataqua River and proceeded into the Atlantic to begin her initial sea trials. Minutes after she nosed into the ocean for her first dive, her engine compartments flooded and she sank, stern-first. Thirty-one men survived but they were entombed in the freezing cold waters off Portsmouth, New Hampshire.

Worse, no one had ever been rescued from a submarine before, and everyone on board knew it. Still, there was hope. A new rescue bell had entered the submarine service, although it had never been used in an actual emergency. Now they had their chance.

The first trick for the rescuers was to find the *Squalus*. In 1939, that was easier said than done. There was virtually no communications device that a submerged submarine could use to talk to a surface ship without a wired connection. The captain did have rockets. They were a type that floated to the surface and then ignited. For several hours, the captain ordered one rocket fired on the hour. But they were difficult to see unless you were close by and for hours, their rockets met only with silence.

On the surface, the ships from Portsmouth were frantically sweeping the seas in the area where *Squalus* dived, and it was indeed the smoke from a rocket that drew them in closer to the spot. They pinged the bottom and the men on the *Squalus* tapped back with an iron hammer against the side of their conning tower to reply. But for some reason their taps were not being heard. Perhaps they were too far down. Perhaps there was a temperature inversion in the ocean waters. Whatever the reason, the clanking of the hammer was not being heard.

As it happened, members of the press were touring the Portsmouth base that morning when the news of the *Squalus* spread around the base. Reporters were on their telephones immediately and in short order the wire services carried the news flash nationwide—the *Squalus* was on the bottom.

Reporters swarmed to Portsmouth and when they got to the docks, they even went so far as to hire fishermen who would take them out to lay beside the rescue ships so they could yell up their questions. Soon the surface was swarming with boats. Unknown to the rescuers, the tired, cold men on the *Squalus* could hear the sonar pinging their ship. In fact, at great expense of energy, they were slamming their sledge-hammer and actively, desperately tapping out their replies. But they weren't being heard. Hours passed and nothing. The ships pinged, the submariners tapped code; no one heard them. But then something happened. Some explain it as a surge of cold water that "opened" up the seas to the sounds from the bottom. Whatever it was, the Morse Code coming from the *Squalus* suddenly rang out crystal clear to the men above.

To the question "How are you?" the *Squalus* hammered its response: "Conditions satisfactory but cold." They intended the message only for their Navy rescuers but taps were loud and clear and heard by all in the area, including the reporters. In an hour, the simple heart-rending words, conditions satisfactory but cold, were flashed across the wire services around the world.

It was probably the least secret message ever sent from one military ship to another, but the effect it had was utterly energizing. Tired as they were, the men on the search-and-rescue vessels doubled their efforts while the world rallied the Navy to spare no expense. Millions prayed and waited.

The prayers were soon answered. Shortly after noon on May 24, the untested rescue bell went down to the bottom and attached to the *Squalus*. Those on the surface waited. The waters were still for several minutes. Then, to a whoosh of bubbles and a whir of cables, the bell began its ascent. The dramatic moment was transmitted live by radio when the bell burst through the surface and was pulled alongside a rescue vessel. As the first of seven rescued seamen emerged and waved his hand, a world cheered through tears of relief.

The rescue may be the first instance of a classic Navy protocol being followed underwater. As the seal was made between the diving bell and the *Squalus*, and the hatch was opened, the operator of the bell uttered those traditional Navy words, "Permission to come aboard, sir."

STOP YOUR SQUAWKING!

Two brothers, Richard and Bob, were flying out to Montana for a hunting trip in Richard's Cessna. Richard was cruising on a northeasterly heading at 7,500 feet, listening to Bob tell him about his expensive new hunting rifle, when the air traffic controller called him and said, "Cessna, your transponder appears to be intermittent; I'm not receiving an altitude readout at this time—confirm your squawk, please."

Richard focused on the altitude readout portion of the controller's call. Thinking that the controller wanted him to verify his altitude, the pilot transmitted, "Roger, I'm squawking 7500."

Of course what Richard meant was that the Mode C portion of his transponder should be transmitting 7,500 feet. But the word "squawk" means something quite different. The controller heard the pilot say that he was "squawking" 7500—meaning that he was trying to use his transponder to send the identifying number string of 7500, a discreet transponder code used to indicate a hijacking!

To make matters worse, just as the pilot made his call, the transponder stopped working completely. Now the only thing the controller had to go on was the radio transmission, and the pilot was telling him that he was trying to squawk 7500.

The pilot did not catch on when the controller asked him to verify that he was squawking 7500. Richard squeezed the microphone and said, "Yes! I'm squawking 7500, don't you read it on your scope?"

The controller took the edgy tone in Richard's voice to be further confirmation that he was a pilot in distress. The controller said, "Be advised that your transponder is completely inoperative at this time, but I copy your transmission that you are squawking 7500. State your intentions, please."

Well, "state your intentions" threw Richard off a bit. He wasn't sure about the legality of flying without a transponder, and he thought the controller's tone made it sound as if he was in trouble. In an effort to feel out the controller's disposition on the subject, Richard radioed, "We have no definite intentions at this time—what do you suggest?"

The controller now thought he was talking to a desperate pilot. Standard procedure called for a vector to an isolated airfield where security forces could subdue the hijacker. "Malmstrom Air Force Base is due east of your location about forty miles. I'm sure that you can obtain the assistance you require there."

Soon Malmstrom was clearing Richard to land. In spite of all the F-111s on the ramp, both Richard and Bob remarked on the noticeable lack of personnel or service vehicles on the ground. They followed a ground controller's instructions, which resulted in a long taxi to a remote hangar at the far end of the field.

Richard shut down the engine and waited for someone to come out of the hangar, but nobody showed. After a few minutes, Richard and Bob decided to wander into the hangar to see if they could find the avionics shop. After just a few steps, Bob became leery about leaving his expensive rifle on the plane. So he retrieved his rifle and threw it over his shoulder, then followed Richard across the tarmac.

As soon as they stepped inside the hangar door they were pinned to the wall. Over a dozen security policemen came out of the woodwork, weapons drawn, and they were all pointed at Richard and Bob!

Needless to say, it was quite late in the day before Richard and Bob were on their way again. They were tired and sore from being face down on the asphalt, but they had a great story to tell. Oh, and the Air Force replaced the blown fuse in the transponder.

18:

CODING OUT LOUD

OFTEN important messages must be transmitted in public spaces, even though they are not meant for public consumption. In such circumstances code is often used to mask the messages. This prevents unwanted panic and needless concern, while in other circumstances it prevents crowds from gathering at the site of an unfolding drama.

"DR. KILDARE TO THE ER, CODE BLUE STAT!"

Hospitals, for example, use their PA systems to broadcast messages that they know will travel thoughout the hospital. To mask their meanings, they use special codes. Is there such a thing as "Code Blue"? Absolutely. It means that there is an emergency under way, and any and all extraordinary measures must be instantly undertaken to save the situation (usually a life). The "Code Blue" team goes into action. (When it's over, a Code Green is broadcast, telling the hospital staff that the emergency is over.)

But there are other codes, too. Anyone who has been in a hospital knows that doctors are often paged, but in the code of hospital communication, some of the names have a special meaning. "Dr. Quick," for instance, is the code alerting security that help is needed for a disorderly situation. "Dr. Kidd" is a code that tells security that a child is missing and may have been abducted from the hospital. "Dr. Wander" is broadcast in a similar situation but when the missing person is an adult. In either case, all the exits are immediately manned and the hospital is searched from top to bottom.

Most hospitals don't rely solely on a Code Blue for all their medical emergencies. In some hospitals, number codes are employed according to the emergency. A Code 300, for instance, means that a patient is in cardiac or respiratory arrest and the Code 300 Team is needed immediately.

Fires are the most difficult of all broadcasts over a public address system. The word "fire" naturally causes panic, and panic will interfere with the response team's ability to deal with the problem. So the typical fire message broadcast in a hospital often sounds rather innocent. One hospital uses the words "Dayton Dowd" to alert the fire safety teams.

In some way, shape, or form, two other codes are used by hospitals. The first alerts the entire medical staff that a major disaster has occurred outside the hospital and that a large number of casualties are on the way in. This is called an "External 6."

The second code alerts the staff to a disaster inside the hospital, one that necessitates an evacuation. This is sometimes called an "Internal 18." This can be caused by a "Dayton Dowd." Of course, there is one code that is welcomed by all—"All clear."

Color Codes

In Alaska, there is a code system used to announce the status of their many active volcanoes. These codes are typically included in the weather reports broadcast by local television and radio stations. During the 1996 eruption of the Pavlof volcano, the codes were used on an almost minute-by-minute basis. On September 16, and continuing through October 18, 1996, Pavlof started to rumble. Hot shafts of steam vented from large cracks in her mantle and small lava flows wound their way down her northern flanks. On October 19, a Code Orange was declared and broadcast, meaning that a volcanic eruption was imminent. On November 4, the situation worsened and the seismic warning was upgraded to a Code Red. By this code, listeners knew that an eruption was in progress and a violent, explosive eruption was imminent. Pavlof was in fact spewing steam and an ash plume was now soaring twenty-five thousand feet into the sky.

Unexpectedly, she calmed down the next day and was downgraded to a Code Orange, and then even further to a Code Yellow. Thus it went until late December, Pavlof flaring up, then calming down, then flaring up again sometimes with fire fountaining, sometimes just ash and steam, marking her mood. Tracking each change, broadcast far and wide, were the codes. Code Green when it seemed dormant, Code Yellow when it was restless, Code Orange when it was active, and Code Red when it was alive.

Of course, a Code Red in Maryland has nothing at all to do with the seismic activity of volcanoes: Broadcast a Code Red there and Marylanders will stay indoors because the ozone levels are high and overall air quality is low. However, be careful; a Code Red broadcast by the United States Naval Academy in Annapolis has nothing at all to do with air quality but is equally important. A Code Red from the Academy means that they are operating under a snow emergency and you should stay at home. Here's what you would hear on the local radio stations (or on your voice mail; the codes are also sent electronically):

THE NAVAL ACADEMY AND ALL ANNAPOLIS AREA COMPLEX ACTIVITIES ARE CLOSED TODAY. ESSENTIAL PERSONNEL ARE REQUIRED TO REPORT ON TIME. CLASSES ARE CANCELED. CODE RED.

Number Codes

Police and fire departments also have codes, but they don't rely on colors, they rely on numbers. The number codes help them communicate quickly, clearly, and with some degree of secrecy. If a patrolman in the Dallas suburb of Arlington broadcasts that he's working an "04" it means he's at the site of a bad accident. If he's "23," he's telling the dispatcher that he's going to get his car washed.

Police number codes differ from state to state, city to city, and neighborhood to neighborhood. In the Dallas–Fort Worth area there are a half-dozen police departments, plus the county sheriffs and the highway patrol, but few of the number codes in that area mean the same thing. A "10-10" broadcast by the county sheriff means he needs assistance, while in neighboring Fort Worth a "10-10" means that the unit is out of service. A "10-54" in the county means that a cow has wandered onto a road and is being stubborn, while a "10-54" in next-door Fort Worth means that a road sign needs repairing. Making it even more confusing, a "10-54" broadcast by the highway patrol means that they are in silent pursuit of another vehicle.

The police also have dispatch codes. A Code 1 means to handle the assignment in a routine fashion, while a Code 2 means that it's an emergency and the unit should get there with lights and sirens on. Code 3 also means that it's an emergency, but to go to the location silently. Code 4 is the most welcome of them all. It means to disregard the previous transmission.

19:

CHEATS AND SCAMS

$\mathbf{W}$AY DOWN DEEP, people have a competitive, avaricious nature. It's part of our embedded survival instinct. So when people get together to play games, even socially, it is not uncommon if Competitive Man comes out. This sometimes leads to cheating, especially when money is involved. While deplorable, this behavior can also be fascinating, as it offers yet another arena for brilliant human ingenuity in the secret message department.

THE TROUBLE WITH BRIDGE PARTNERS

Of all the card games in the world, bridge is the one in which partners cheat the least, because bridge is such a precise game that it is too easy to spot unusual runs of luck or unorthodox plays that result in a win. Especially at the professional level, bidding that goes wildly against the odds but still wins is automatically a red flag. But down at the neighborhood level, it is not entirely unknown that a little fudging of the rules takes place. It is awfully tempting to nudge your partner into playing the cards you want him to by a gesture, or a sigh, or wiggling in your chair, or a certain eye movement. Any form of secret messaging between partners is, of course, illegal, but some people can't help themselves. Every bridge club includes partners who have predetermined signals. Those coughs, yawns, foot taps, and rapid eye blinks probably mean something.

But experts say it is more difficult to cheat successfully in bridge than it is to simply learn to play better. The Marx Brothers, inveterate and mischievous bridge players in Hollywood, tried to win a tournament once by using a scheme called the "one under one" system, in which a spade bid really means a heart, a no-trump bid means a spade, and so forth. George Burns related that "before the evening was through they were so confused they didn't know what they were doing. They were the first ones eliminated!" But that didn't stop Groucho. He once told a new partner, "If you like my lead, don't bother to signal with a high card. Just smile and nod your head."

But even in friendly games good players have a sixth sense about secret messages at the table. The famous Charles Goren is said to have once played with a woman who was waiting to hurl a trump on the next spade lead. Goren led a diamond, and the disappointed lady twitched noticeably in her chair. He led another diamond and her twitch turned into a violent shake. "Ma'am," Goren said, "you've got to stop that. It makes for a bad partnership. And besides, I don't have any more spades!"

When money and international prestige are involved, cheating has been known to occur. As in casual games, the method involves covert communication between partners, but the pros are more subtle, and certainly more careful than most. Usually the signaling is done at the beginning of the game, to suggest an opening bid or to indicate the pattern of cards held in one's hand.

An Austrian team was caught once at an international tournament using this system: A strong hand was expressed by a clenched fist on the table; a flat hand indicated a poor one; the ace of clubs was held vertically in the right hand; the ace of spades was held at a forty-five-degree angle; the aces of diamonds and hearts rested on the table horizontally; pencils and cigarettes placed in certain predetermined positions indicated virtually every possible option of play. They were caught, of course, and suspended from tournament bridge, but how many tournaments had they played in which they weren't caught?

In 1965, a bridge scandal erupted with such drama that it was given a name worthy of an action movie: The Buenos Aires Affair. The British team of Terence Reese and Boris Shapiro were accused of using finger signals during an international tournament in Buenos Aires. They were observed by several people, including the bridge columnist for *The New York Times*, to be holding their cards in an inconsistent way. That is, they would vary the number of fingers showing at the back of the hand, and would close or open the fingers from hand to hand. It was alleged that these were signals indicating how many hearts they held—two fingers showing meant either two hearts or five hearts (fingers open on the first, closed on the latter), three fingers for three hearts or six, and so on.

This is the kind of secret message that would work perfectly well around the kitchen table, but in tournament bridge the inconsistent position of the fingers was spotted readily. The players sputtered their innocence, but the World Bridge Federation ultimately decided they were guilty.

Another notorious scandal occurred ten years later, and it, too, was given a juicy name: The Bermuda Incident. Observed by an American journalist, an Italian player was apparently signaling his partner by means of foot taps under the table. The journalist informed the non-playing captain of the North American team, Alfred (Freddy) Sheinwold, who, appropriately, had been the chief of codes and ciphers for the OSS during World War II. Who better to spot a secret message? After an executive committee made their suspicions known to the players, they protested their innocence. One of the Italians said it was just "nervous tension" that caused his foot to tap his partner's. The inquiry was inconclusive, with such experts as Oswald Jacoby saying that he could not perceive an improvement in play attributable to the alleged foot signals.

But the consensus among the players was that they were guilty, and the other teams, especially Sheinwold's North American team, refused to play the Italians if the two accused men were inserted in the lineup for the finals. The Italians did, in fact, put the alleged cheaters in to play, and the American Contract Bridge League then had to force Sheinwold's team to participate. As it turned out, the Italians played miserably with the besmirched pair, and fell almost hopelessly behind. Ironically, it was only after they were replaced that the Italians made a miraculous rally and won the tournament!

A BLACKJACK SCAM

Never say never, but it is virtually impossible to pull off a successful scam at a casino for very long. The "eyes in the sky" see everything, and they are augmented by teams of professional "scam-spotters" who have a lot of experience. But greed often overcomes common sense, and teams of scam artists try to bilk the casinos every day. Many ruses involve teams of conspirators, who use various signaling systems to co-ordinate their movements.

One of the tricks is the blackjack scam. This involves two or more people, and one of them has to be a crooked dealer. The dealer, who knows better than anyone how rigorous the scrutiny is, thinks he has found a way to slip his buddy a fifty- or hundred-dollar chip. It starts this way: His confederate, posing as a player, steps up behind the seated players at the dealer's table and mills around a bit. That is his signal to the dealer to start the play. The player has a dark-colored drink in his hand, probably a Coca-Cola, with no ice. He holds it out in front of him, and as he sits down at the table, he places his drink well forward, all the way into the "play" area in front of the dealer. The dealer apologizes and tells the man that his drink must be placed closer in front of him. The dealer reaches for the glass, holding it at the top, with his palm facing the contents of the glass. The glass is moved back a few inches. The player then plays, busts, and leaves the table.

He probably heads for a bathroom stall, where behind the locked door he reaches his fingers into his drink and pulls out a dark-blue chip, perfectly hidden by the liquid. The dealer had dropped it into his glass as he moved it back toward the player.

20:

SIGNS AND SYMBOLS

Is THERE ANYONE IN THE WORLD who does not understand that a red circle with a red diagonal line through it means, "Do not" or "No . . ." (No smoking, No parking, and so forth)? This was not a conventional symbol fifty years ago; why do we understand it so well now? Because of usage. In time all symbols become familiar, and the messages they deliver in shorthand become second nature.

Graphic representations—lines, squares, triangles, circles, and so forth—have the ability to communicate and memorialize concepts, give directions, and in very artful configurations, even express human emotions.

WHAT IS THE MESSAGE, O GREAT SEAL?

The American one-dollar bill features on one side the Great Seal of the United States, which is shown on the left and right sides of the bill. At first glance it is clear that the principal image on the left is a pyramid; on the right is an eagle. But a close examination shows that the Great Seal is much more—a dense mixture of images and inscriptions that are complex enough to suggest that the composition sends a message, as all good symbols do.

If we assume that each object is included for a reason, what did the designers of the Great Seal intend for it to say?

We know that the founding fathers (Washington, Jefferson, Adams, et al.) were Freemasons, and the pyramid is an important symbol in Masonic mythology. Joseph Campbell, student and teacher of myth, suggests in his book *The Power of Myth* that the pyramid was borrowed from that tradition, but that it also symbolizes the four points of the compass from which America draws its citizens. The rise and convergence of the pyramid's geometry at the top point further symbolizes a Jeffersonian ideal—that at the bottom of the pyramid we are separate, alone, and different, but as we ascend, through reason, we come together at the top, where there are no sides. The eye at the top of the pyramid is the eye of pure reason, the fundamental enabler of a democratic society.

Proving that no artistic detail is beyond the assignment of symbolism, there are thirteen levels of the pyramid, an obvious reference to the original thirteen states. At the bottom (the beginning, as it were) is inscribed MDCCLXXVI—the year 1776, the year of the Declaration of Independence. For those who believe in such things, both numbers have numerological significance beyond the obvious. Thirteen is the number of transformation and rebirth, demonstrated in such places as the Last Supper (Christ and his twelve disciples), and the zodiac (one number just beyond, thus transcending, the twelve sun signs). Further (no groaning, please), the sum of 1, 7, 7, and 6 is 21, the age of the birth of reason.

Above the pyramid is written Annuit Coeptis, a lift from Virgil's *Aeneid*, which can be translated from the Latin as, "He smiles on our beginnings," an affirmation from the founding fathers that they were following a divine plan in establishing a country based on democracy and freedom. Below the pyramid is inscribed "Novus Ordo Seclorum"—"A New Order of the Ages [is created]." Over on the other side, the eagle must have been chosen for its traditional symbolism as a manifestation of God on earth. This is Zeus's bird, with its wings outstretched, just as it is often depicted on Roman shields and battle flags. But this eagle has a duality. It is capable of war or peace, both symbolized by the objects it holds in its talons. To the right it holds thirteen arrows, symbols of war. To the left it holds a laurel branch, traditional symbol of peace, with thirteen leaves. Significantly, the eagle looks in the direction of peace, as if to indicate its ideals and hopes, while holding the tools of war in reserve.

A MESSAGE IN THE MARKS

For the Native American tribes of the Plains—including the Comanches, the Sioux, the Blackfeet, the Crow, the Cheyenne, and many others—the horse was supremely important. It was an indispensable animal for hunting, for war, for games, and for entertainment. The warrior and his horse were one. And as the warrior painted himself to indicate to others his prowess in war, so he painted his horse, too. There were traditional symbols painted on the neck and flanks of the horse to communicate to enemies just how many times the horse and rider had fought in combat, and what had happened to their enemies. The overall idea was to decorate the horse ferociously, and to send an ominous visual message.

Some of the symbols and their meanings:

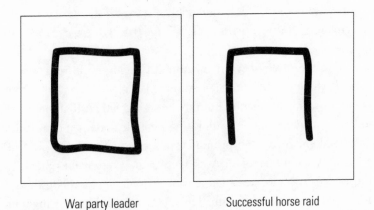

War party leader   Successful horse raid

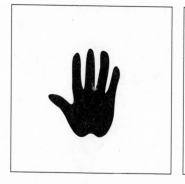

Killed a man in combat

"Coup" marks

THE LANGUAGE OF CATTLE BRANDS

Branding cattle to indicate ownership was originally a Spanish idea brought to the vast expanse of the American West. The idea was sound—branding was the only way to safeguard four-legged property in the early, lawless West—but the forms and symbols used as brands grew haphazardly and without official registration; often the marks were designed by cowboys sitting around the campfire with a stick in the dirt. But there developed a kind of logic and uniformity to the practice over time. The brands that started to appear on cattle were as rich and unfettered as the land they came from, but there were language rules that dictated how you read the symbols. For example:

Two Bar X

Circle R

Then there were added some qualifying prefix symbols, such as:

Lazy R   Crazy R   Rocking R   Flying R

Other prefixes include Tumbling, Walking, Running, Swinging, Barbed, Reverse, Diamond, Box, and Broken. The cowboys who roamed the West were familiar with these symbols and what they meant, spoke of them at roundups and drives, and generally kept a mental list of what brands belonged to whom. But by the late 1800s the number of ranches and brands became too numerous to organize without paper and pencil. Soon all brands were required by state law to be registered, and state "brand books" began to be printed every year.

This imposition of bureaucracy, fortunately, did not stop ranchers from inventing a wide variety of humorous and cautionary brands, whose meanings are sometimes mysterious without a translation:

I-U

A direct message to rustlers—I Bar You (variation: ICU for I See You).

.45

An even stronger message—Colt Forty-Five.

Obviously, a name in a brand—Barker.

S R

Other names—Keys   Harter

P

Perhaps won in a card game? Seven-Up.

NO

Or another gambling game? Keno.

So YOU SURVIVED A SHIPWRECK?

It all goes back to George Washington, and he would be proud.

Do you know that it is possible to discern the high points of a person's career even if you've never read about the person, never heard about him, or even met him before? It's not mentalism, but rather the secret messages of military ribbons. By merely glancing at a uniform one can "read" a person's entire resume. The ribbons affixed to the left breast of a military uniform can tell you where that person lives, what his unit is, what special training he has had, if and where he served in combat, that he is an expert with a rifle, cherishes good values, landed as part of an invasion force, flew during the Berlin Air Lift—or even was on a ship that sank. All this comes from "reading" the messages of the ribbons.

One of the underlying concepts of a military organization is to minimize the development of close personal friendships. Why? It's actually a practical matter. If a friend is wounded in combat, experience shows that two friends will stop to help, which, of course, has the undesired effect of taking three people out of the battle. Multiply this by several injuries and you could quickly incapacitate an entire platoon.

To prevent this from happening, the military keeps its people moving. Every two or three years, one will receive a new assignment and will move to a new base or even to a new part of the world. Friendship bonds are thus weakened, but this does tend to create a military of strangers—and therein lies the utility of the ribbons. The ribbons bridge the gap. Whenever two military men or women meet, they can quickly size each other up and determine what common bonds they have simply by reading the ribbons.

Which, in fact, is exactly what was intended in the beginning—for a commander to be able to tell, at a glance, what skills his subordinates have.

Today, the use of ribbons has spread beyond the Army, Navy, Marines, and Air Force. City police forces, fire-fighting forces, even the Boy Scouts use ribbons and badges to communicate a person's resume.

But what does this have to do with George Washington? Following the Revolutionary War, the Continental Congress bestowed medals upon three of its heroes—General Horatio Gates, Captain John Paul Jones, and General George Washington. Later, as president, Washington decreed that military valor and merit should be recognized through a system of medals and ribbons. He started it with something called the Military Badge of Merit. The Military Badge of Merit was a medal, shaped like a heart, with the word "Merit" across the front. It was to be worn over the left breast, made out of cloth or silk, purple in color, edged with lace.

Unfortunately, after some initial but brief pomp, it quickly fell into disuse. In fact, the medal would have disappeared entirely were it not for General Douglas MacArthur. MacArthur restored the award in 1932, but not as the Badge of Merit. Owing to its shape and the color, it was obvious to call it the Purple Heart. It would forever mark the wearer as a combat veteran who sustained an injury in battle.

What Washington began in 1782 flourishes today. As of 1998, the military had eighty-one awards that are to be worn on a uniform, with seventy-seven specific attachments. Each attachment, too, tells a story. How do you know someone survived a sinking? Because there is a small star attached to the ribbon of the sea service medal.

21:

THE SECRET MESSAGE MYSTERIES

SECRET MESSAGES don't always work. Why? It is not unheard of for a secret message to be misunderstood (as we have seen in earlier chapters) or to defy translation altogether. Ancient writings often fall into the latter category. It wasn't until the middle of the nineteenth century, after all, that the keys to unraveling the Egyptian hieroglyphs were discovered.

Some ancient writings have never been translated. The signs, symbols, and letter forms of which they are composed have no recognizable roots or references that any modern scholar can use as a starting point for investigation. These will probably always be mysteries. It just goes to show how easy it is to lose word and symbol "keys" over time. Here is one story that proves that idea; one that illustrates code ineptitude; and one gloriously inventive message that may turn out to be a secret despite all our best intentions to make it manifest to the cosmos.

THE SECRET MESSAGE OF DIGHTON ROCK

Dighton is an old New England village on the Taunton River at Assonet Neck. It is in the New Bedford/Fall River area of Massachusetts, famous for its sailing and commercial fishing. But for over three hundred years it has been a magnet for people curious about a rock—a boulder, really—eleven feet long and five feet high, on which someone, at some early time in history (perhaps pre-Columbus), carved a message that has been one of the great enigmas in American history. Running the length of the rock are lines, shapes, symbols, and letters that seem organized and planned, as if to send a message, but one whose meaning has eluded researchers, historians, and amateur theorists for over three centuries.

Now called the Dighton Rock, the carved boulder sat at the water's edge, facing outward, leading most theorists to believe that the message, whatever it is, was intended to be seen by explorers plying the Taunton River.

Cotton Mather mentions it in *The Wonderful Works of God Commemorated in 1690*: ". . . a mighty Rock . . . deeply engraved, no man alive knows How or When about half a score Lines, near Ten Foot Long, and a foot and a half broad, filled with strange Characters; which would suggest as odd Thoughts about them that were here before us . . ."

There is no doubt about certain things: 1) The inscription on the rock is not of recent origin. In addition to the Mather citation, a Reverend John Danforth sketched the inscription in 1680 (his drawing now resides in the British Museum); 2) the lines and symbols were carved by men, not the forces of nature; 3) the lines must have a meaning, because the labor required to execute the design must have been enormous. Idle rock chiseling could have been accomplished on a smaller scale, and in a much more accessible place.

What do the carvings on the rock mean, then? There is no shortage of hypotheses, but some interesting ones are:

- A 1781 opinion from a French count declared it a message from ancient Carthaginians who had reached the New World and lived briefly on Mount Hope Bay.

- A schoolteacher in 1831 claimed it was a message left by Phoenician explorers from Tyre, the lines describing their route from the eastern Mediterranean past Gibraltar and the Canary Islands, and across the Atlantic Ocean.

- A Danish scholar named Rafn seemed to have solved the puzzle in 1837. He claimed it was a depiction of the travels of Norse explorer Thorfinn Karlsefne, as unearthed in Icelandic manuscripts and supported by popular Norse myth. He went so far as to declare Dighton the place called Hop in the Norse legend, where Karlsefne's son was born. The characters, he said, were runic and spelled out the words "Nam Thorfins." To those who believed that Viking explorers reached North America long before Columbus, this was proof positive. But Brown University professor Edward Delabarre discredited the Rafn theory by proving, in 1916, that Rafn had doctored the sketches of the inscription with additional lines and symbols to support his case.

Delebarre's own interpretation at first was that the lines were meaningless carved doodles left by Native Americans. But one day, while staring at a photograph of the rock, he clearly saw a date: 1511. Then he claimed to see the shield of the Kingdom of Portugal and a name—Miguel Cortereal. After a bit of investigation he learned that Cortereal was a Portuguese explorer who had reached Newfoundland in 1502, and had subsequently vanished. Perhaps his ship had sunk, leaving him stranded for nine years. Was the 1511 inscription on the rock a desperate SOS to passing ships?

While initially popular in Portugal, Delabarre's conclusion has by no means been accepted universally. Casual observers fail to see any of the names or dates cited by Delabarre, or anyone else for that matter. But everyone loves a puzzle, and there are hundreds of wild speculations continuing to this day. The experts now agree, though—the keys to solving the riddle of the Dighton Rock are in our distant past, hidden by time, and will always remain a secret.

THE MONGOOSE MESSAGES

The United States submarine surfaced near the Cuban shoreline and began to transmit its message: "The fish will rise very soon." To Cubans who heard this over Radio Free Cuba the message was ambiguous. It sounded as if something big was going to happen, but what? Are we the fish, they thought? And why are the fish rising—are they dead?

The CIA, which operated the clandestine radio station from the submarine, had devised this secret message as a rousing call to arms, but here, on the eve of the invasion of Cuba at the Bay of Pigs, the message was laying an egg. There was no civil uprising, no marching in the street. The psychological warfare (PSWAR) group operating under the general directive (PSYOP) known as Operation Mongoose had obviously failed to light a fire under the Cuban people. They had tried for months to find an effective propaganda symbol and theme for the anti-Castro movement, and had only come up with this weak "fish" line.

What about "worm" instead of "fish," they wondered? Castro had called his political opponents gusanos—worms. By late 1962 the CIA inserted the slogan "Gusano Libre!" (Free Worm) in its Radio Free Cuba broadcasts. They were dismayed to find that this, too, had no revolutionary power as a call to arms. In October 1962 the Cuban Missile Crisis effectively ended Operation Mongoose, but the anti-Castro psywar continued into 1963. When the Kennedy administration's secret support of the CIA's exile front group, the Cuban Revolutionary Council (CRC), was terminated, the Mongoose-era holdovers thought the time was right for a new anti-Castro leader. What they wanted was a dashing, romantic Latin leader, tough, anticommunist, populist, small in stature but big in heart. Where would they find such a person? They couldn't. So they invented him. They created an entire history of an imaginary leader, complete with tales of daring exploits against Castro's goons. The psywar experts worked on a codename, which they hoped the Cuban people would whisper reverently, hopefully. How about "The Little Worm," they mused? Or "The Friendly Worm"? Or "The Fighting Friend"?

This plan never got out of the proposal stage, but it promised to be as desultory as the "fish" and the "worm" and the other secret message parts of Operation Mongoose that preceded it.

In the forty years since "Mongoose," the Cuban government has survived all U.S. political propaganda adventures. But at the millennium (as we write), Cuba is about to fall under the weight of America's global cultural juggernaut. What psywar experts could not do in the 1960s is now being done by music, movies, sports, fashion, and television (without the aid of secret messages!).

THE VOYNICH MANUSCRIPT

William Voynich, an American antiquarian book dealer, found the book of a lifetime in a neglected storeroom of an Italian school in 1912. It was a small, untitled manuscript of medieval origin, whose two hundred thick pages of vellum contained writings in black ink and vivid color illustrations of plants and flowers. Voynich soon realized that what he thought were sentences in Latin or some other language were not sentences at all. Or rather, they were sentences whose letters bore no resemblance to any language Voynich had ever seen. This was obviously a book written in code, and Voynich sent copies of it to professional cryptanalysts in hopes of getting a key to deciphering it.

News of the book's existence spread quickly to cryptanalysts around the world, who to a person were deeply mystified by the strange letter forms and their connections to the pictures. The more they studied it, the more frustrated they became. Not one person, using the full arsenal of modern code-breaking techniques, could make a dent in the mystery. And they still haven't. The manuscript now is kept in the Beineke Library at Yale University, as impenetrable today as it was on the day Voynich found it. Except for one sentence. It is on the final page of the book, and it is the only sentence in the entire book written with recognizable Latin letters. It reads: "Michiton oladabas multos te fecr cerc portas." In itself this makes no sense. But a professor named

William Newbold in 1921 factored out the possible nulls [letters with no meaning] and came up with this Latin sentence: "A mihi dabas multos portas" — "You have given me many gates."

This is the kind of titillating clue that could spur the patient and tenacious fraternity of cryptanalysts to work for centuries. And they may need it. As much as they hate an unsolved puzzle, this one may stump them for all time.

22:

WORD PLAY

Anagrams, puns, acrostics, palindromes—word play is the very stuff from which secret messages are constructed. Codebreakers, they say, fall into two camps—the numbers people and the word people. Here are five stories from the word people, featuring the inventive use of letters and language to create amusing, fascinating, and clever secret messages.

The victor hugo message

Extreme brevity can be a type of code. Shortened words, unfinished sentences, abbreviations, and acronyms are often used in written correspondence or in conversations between two parties who know each other very well. An outsider who overhears rarely "gets" the message.

There must have been just that sort of sympathetic communication at work when Victor Hugo cabled his English publisher, eager to know whether the translation of *Les Miserables* was going over well with the public. The book had been a sensation all over Europe, so Hugo must have been confident of its success. But, not wanting to show any anxiety, his unsigned cable to his publisher read:

"?"

Days later, his prescient publisher, who understood this secret message, replied:

"!"

in surely the briefest telegraphic correspondence in history (documented in the *Guinness Book of Records*).

WORD PLAY FROM VOLTAIRE

The French philosopher Voltaire exhibited a lifelong sense of humor that buoyed him when deeper, darker thoughts threatened to wear him down. Indeed, he is considered the wittiest man in an age of great wit. His fierce comedy could appear in long forms, like the comic novel *Candide,* or in toss-off amusements, like this exchange with his patron, Frederick the Great of Prussia. Wishing to have Voltaire come for dinner, Frederick wrote to him:

P
Venez

Days passed. By return courier, a letter arrived for Frederick from Voltaire. He opened the letter and read:

J/a

Upon reading this he smiled, and called out to his servants, "Let's prepare! The great Voltaire is coming to dinner!"

How did he know this? For that matter, how did Voltaire decipher the odd word arrangement he received in the first place?

Both bits of clever, coded communication are rebuses. They were created in fun, as a word game between two intelligent men, but they stand as good examples of how mental ingenuity can create fascinating secret messages. Frederick's original invitation was quite a brainteaser. Voltaire first recognized a French word, venez (the imperative, come). But why was the letter P stacked on top of it? It soon came to him. The word venez was under the letter "P." The letter P in French is pronounced "pay." The word for "under" in French is sous. So the line reads, in French, "Venez sous p" (venez under p), which is a homonym for "Venez souper," which means (aha!), "Come for dinner!" Apparently amused, Voltaire composed his reply as a return brainteaser—capital J, lowercase a, or, put another way, Big J, small a. In French that's J grand, a petit. It hit Frederick in a flash—J'ai grand appetit! (I'm hungry!) That's how he knew Voltaire was on his way.

Lewis in Wonderland

The incomparable Lewis Carroll was one of the English language's most adroit and frisky practitioners, equally at home with puns, palindromes, riddles, acrostics, and other word games. History will remember him most for *Through the Looking Glass*, a work replete with wordplay and inside jokes. There are secret messages galore within, but one of them stands out. Right at the end, in a burst of beautiful verse, Carroll makes a sentimental reference to the day in July (of 1862) when he started telling the "Alice in Wonderland" stories to the three Liddell sisters, daughters of a friend. In these seven stanzas Carroll hides a loving and sentimental acrostic nod to Alice Pleasance Liddell, who was the model for the Alice character:

A BOAT, BENEATH A SUNNY SKY
LINGERING ONWARD DREAMILY
IN AN EVENING OF JULY—

CHILDREN THREE THAT NESTLE NEAR,
EAGER EYE AND WILLING EAR,
PLEASED A SIMPLE TALE TO HEAR—

LONG HAS PALED THAT SUNNY SKY;
ECHOES FADE AND MEMORIES DIE;
AUTUMN FROSTS HAVE SLAIN JULY.

STILL SHE HAUNTS ME, PHANTOMWISE,
ALICE MOVING UNDER SKIES
NEVER SEEN BY WAKING EYES.

CHILDREN YET, THE TALE TO HEAR,
EAGER EYE AND WILLING EAR,
LOVINGLY SHALL NESTLE NEAR.

IN A WONDERLAND THEY LIE,
DREAMING AS THE DAYS GO BY,
DREAMING AS THE SUMMERS DIE;

EVER DRIFTING DOWN THE STREAM—
LINGERING IN THE GOLDEN GLEAM—
LIFE, WHAT IS IT BUT A DREAM?

THE SECRET OF SPACE

Although they would not fool professional cryptologists (not for long, anyway), simple hidden-word techniques have been found useful for writing secret messages. One method involves hiding words within sentences. If you were a spy, for example, and wanted to know where to go for your next assignment, your superiors might cable you this message: "Drop Aristotle book at the library." Within the sentence lies a city—Paris.

Perhaps the easiest way to hide a written message is to change the spacing between the letters of a sentence. A hastily written sign attached to a hitching post in a country town proves the point. The sign read, "TOTI EMU LESTO," and had people scratching their heads for days. There was nothing to do but ask the storeowner what the heck it meant. "Just trying to be helpful," he said. "I wanted people to know that the post was there to tie mules to."

ALEXANDER THE GREAT GETS THE MESSAGE

As Alexander the Great's Macedonian army struggled for six months to breach the walls of the Phoenician port city of Tyre, his sleep was fitful. In a dream, the image of an unusual beast came to him. It appeared to be a man but had the ears and tail of a horse. It danced in riotous circles around him. The next day, Alexander's adviser Aristander, on hearing the recounting of the dream, proclaimed it to be a secret message from the gods, a good omen on the eve of battle. The beast, he said, was a satyr, a sylvan deity. The word "satyr" in Greek is spelled Σατρος. Aristander spotted a secret message within the word. He added a space between the second and the third letters to create two words, Σα προς. The new meaning? "Tyre is yours." And the next day, so the tale goes, it was. The walls came tumbling down, and Alexander, in a vengeful mood, ordered the slaughter and crucifixion of some twenty thousand men.

23:

IN PLAIN SIGHT

THE WORLD OF ART AND ILLUSTRATION offers a wide palette for hiding secret messages. Words or images can be hidden within the work, or the whole composition can be a message in disguise.

MARRY ME!

If you are a regular reader of the *Louisville Courier-Journal*, you know about Nick Anderson and Colton.

Anderson is the newspaper's award-winning political cartoonist. His detailed drawings are works of art, combining complex line work with a keen view of the news landscape and a politically tart tongue. But, as much as everyone admires his artistic ability and his editorial zingers, the thing that causes thousands of Kentuckians to peer closely at his cartoons every day is the search for "Colton."

You see, starting from the day his son Colton was born, Anderson started blending Colton's name into the line art of his cartoons, just as his predecessor at the newspaper, Hugh Haynie, had done with his wife's name—Lois. Anderson hides "Colton" in President Clinton's hair, or in Boris Yeltin's belt, or in the withers of a Kentucky Derby horse.

What few people know, however, is that Anderson actually started his playful messaging with the name Cecilia. One day, in a cartoon that used a bride and groom as an artistic theme, he concealed a secret message in the ruffles on the sleeve of the bride's dress. It said, "Marry me, Cecilia," in perhaps one of the most unique marriage proposals in journalism history.

Of course, Anderson didn't want this message to be too well hidden. Can you find it as easily as Cecilia Anderson, mother of Colton, did?

THE LEPIDOPTERA MESSAGE

At first glance the man looked like an eccentric butterfly collector— pith helmet, thick eyeglasses, short pants, and a butterfly net that he swung awkwardly as he dashed around the meadow. To the German soldiers stationed at the nearby fort, the sight of the Englishman

Robert Baden-Powell collecting butterfly specimens was laughable, and certainly no threat. For several days in 1891 Baden-Powell had chased butterflies all the way around the fort, stopping every hour to make sketches of the specimens he had caught. His notebook was filled with them. If anyone ever asked to see his work, Baden-Powell was only too happy to oblige. His artwork of butterflies and insects was not professional caliber, but decent for an amateur, with all the important spots and markings included.

It was twenty-five years later, upon publication of his book *My Adventures as a Spy*, that the world finally learned the truth—that Baden-Powell was not some harmless, doddering naturalist, but a very clever and very successful spy for the British army. Disguised within those sketches of butterflies in 1891 were indications of the size and shape of the fort and the position of all its gun emplacements.

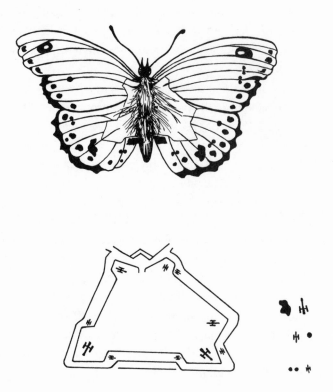

The large dots that look like wing colorations are the locations of the fort's main guns; the smaller black dots show the locations of field artillery and machine-gun emplacements.

After many years of service of this type, Baden-Powell wrote a small book called *Aids for Scouting*, which the army used as a training manual for its scouts and trackers. It soon came to Baden-Powell's attention that the book was enjoying a wider application than he had intended—as a "skills and fitness" training course for schoolboys in England and South Africa. Recognizing a need, Baden-Powell set about writing a proper book, and the result was *Scouting for Boys*, the seminal work that brought about the movement Sir Robert Baden-Powell is legendary for today—the Boy Scouts.

Corporal Violet

The defiant Napoleon Bonaparte, abdicating and going into exile on the island of Elba off the Tuscan coast of Italy in 1814, assured his loyal followers with the following words: I will return, he said, "in the violet season."

From that moment on the violet became the symbol among pro-Bonaparte factions of the hoped-for Napoleonic return to power. His followers secretly identified each other by wearing bunches of violets in their lapels. Their name for Napoleon became "Corporal Violet."

This drawing was printed in 1815, just as Napoleon escaped Elba and returned to France, hoping to regain his empire. It seems innocuous enough. It appears to be just a picture of flowers. But look at it carefully. Within the leaves and stems of the violets you will find a carefully camouflaged left profile of Napoleon, facing a right profile of his second wife, Marie Louise, and below them a right profile of their son, Napoleon II, the young king of Rome.

Ironically, by the time this drawing was made, Napoleon had not seen his wife and son for almost a year, and never would again. In 1815 they had fled to Austria, and Napoleon, having been defeated at Waterloo, was held in captivity by the British on the island of Saint Helena until his death in 1821.

24:

WRITE ME A LETTER

INTERCEPTING AND READING someone else's mail has been a crude but effective way of gathering intelligence for thousands of years. But there have been plenty of clever ways of disguising secret messages within letters. Here are stories that show how easily it can be done.

THE TIC-TAC-TOE SYSTEM

There have always been secret methods of communication within prison communities. Techniques run the gamut of possibilities, from sign language to invented languages to coded, written messages. Of the three types, written messages are the most vulnerable to interception and decoding by authorities, because someone, somewhere, has to be in possession of the "key"—the instructions, so to speak, of the method of encryption. If guards can capture the key, they can read the messages.

The so-called "Tic-Tac-Toe" system has been a mainstay code writing system within prison populations for years. Every so often a variation pops up, but the examples below demonstrate the variety of ways the strategy game Tic-Tac-Toe can be used to create a serviceable code system.

THE BASIC TIC-TAC-TOE CODE

This is a clever code that uses the familiar grid lines of a Tic-Tac-Toe game as substitutes for letters. It starts with an arrangement of the entire alphabet into two Tic-Tac-Toe grids and two diagonal variations on the grid, with dots strategically placed as shown.

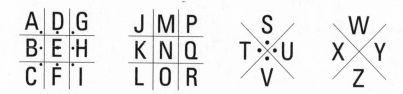

The key to understanding the system is found not in the letters themselves but in the geometric configuration of the grid lines and the position of the dots. These are used as substitutes for the letters that reside in the grid. In this way the letter A becomes ⌐, B becomes ⌐, and so on.

"Breakout tonight" becomes:

This is an effective code because it is easy for first-timers to use, and is simple enough to memorize, eliminating the need to have a written code key lying around. Its weakness is its simplicity, too. Once discovered, it is no longer useful. That's why variations were developed, just to keep authorities on their toes. Simply moving the location of the dots offers a number of variations, such as this one confiscated from a Mexican Mafia member:

The use of symbols rather than dots gives the code a different twist:

```
A D G      J M P      S V Y
B E H      K N Q      T W Z
C F I      L O R      U X
```

Finally, a degree of difficulty can be imposed by the prisoners' occasional switch or rotation of the symbols in the middle of a coded message.

Today's convict population might be surprised to learn that this code system has been around for centuries. It is often called the Pigpen Code, so named because of the rectilinear arrangement that resembles the fences in a hog lot. The Freemasons used the Pigpen system to encrypt the details of their financial transactions in the 1700s, and variations of the system have been handed down over hundreds of years in many British public schools.

THE SPOKEN TIC-TAC-TOE CODE

To communicate verbally in code (a handy skill when you're yelling from one end of the cell block to the other), prisoners in various populations have devised a number substitution code based on Tic-Tac-Toe. It is a variation of the simplest number substitution code known to man: 1 equals A, 2 equals B, and so on. The Tic-Tac-Toe grid is simply used to reorder the alphabet as shown below:

1	4	7		10	13	16			19			23	
A	B	C		D	E	F			S			W	
2	5	8		11	14	17		20 U	T 22		24 X	Y 26	
G	H	I		J	K	L			V			Z	
3	6	9		12	15	18			21			25	
M	N	O		P	Q	R							

So when a convict wants to express himself, he simply yells, "22-5-13-23-1-18-10-13-6-8-19-1-11-13-18-14!" (We'll let you figure it out.)

THE CLOCK CODE

This code method is yet another variation on the Tic-Tac-Toe theme, but uses a designated time of day to guide the encryption. To make the system work, the sender starts by declaring a start time; let's say twelve noon. That means that, in a circle around the grid, the first letter of the alphabet will be placed in the top center position. All the other letters follow in the normal sequence in a clockwise manner, with the last two letters placed in the center. Here is how it would look:

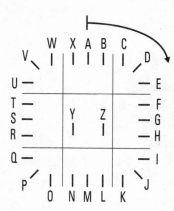

As in the other Tic-Tac-Toe codes, the letter substitutions are then derived from the geometry of the grid and the marks inside the grid lines. "Hello" would be:

The beauty of this code system lies in its versatility. The configuration of the grid lines and marks changes every time the start time changes. If the start time was declared to be nine o'clock instead of noon, the new grid would look like this:

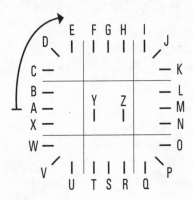

And "hello" would become:

THE WAY OUT SECRET

An old spy-service story has it that during the seventeenth-century English civil wars, monarchist Sir John Trevanian was arrested and sentenced to death. While awaiting execution, Trevanian was locked in infamous Colchester Castle. One day, a letter arrived for him from his servant. It was intercepted and read by the jailers. Seeing nothing to worry about in the correspondence, they passed it on to the doomed man. The letter read:

> Worthie Sir John:-Hope, that is the best comfort of the afflicted,
> cannot much, I fear me, help you now. That I would saye to you, is
> this only: if ever I may be able to requite that I do owe you, stand not
> upon asking me: Tis not much I can do: but what I can do, bee you
> verie sure I wille. I knowe that, if deathe comes, if ordinary men fear

it, it frights not you, accounting it for a high hounour, to have such a rewarde of your loyalty. Pray yet that you may be spare this soe bitter, cup, I fear not that you will grudge any sufferings; onlie if bie submission you can turn them away, this is the part of a wise man. Tell me, as if you can, to do for you anythinge that you can wolde have done. The general goes back on Wednesday. Restinge your servant to command. R.J.

Upon finishing the letter, Sir John asked to go to the chapel to pray before his execution. His guards granted the wish, and waited outside the chapel at the only exit. After an hour they grew suspicious. They raced into the room and found it completely empty. Sir John was gone!

They should have examined the letter more closely. It contains a cleverly concealed message that told Sir John how to escape. Start by selecting the third letter after each punctuation mark. By the end of the letter you'll see the real message:

"Panel at east end of chapel slides."

Armed with this information, Trevanian had found the secret panel in the chapel wall and made his escape.

THE DOUBLE-SIDED MESSAGE

This clever message is attributed to Cardinal Richelieu, who supposedly sent it to the French ambassador in Rome concerning a Benedictine friar, Monsieur Compigne. Historians today doubt the whole story. No matter. Richelieu or not, the writer displays a wickedly adroit vocabulary, and knowledge of a word-spacing technique that allows the letter to be read in two different ways. The gullible friar probably thought the cardinal was being too kind. He wasn't. Here is the original letter:

M. Compigne, a Savoyard by birth, a Friar of the Order of Saint Benedict,
is the man who will present to you as his passport to your protection,

this letter. He is one of the most discreet, the wisest and the least

meddling persons that I have ever known or have had the pleasure to converse with.

He has long earnestly solicited me to write to you in his favor, and

To give him a suitable character, together with a letter of credence;

Which I have accordingly granted to his real merit, rather I must say, than to

His importunity; for, believe me, sir, his modesty is only exceeded by his worth.

I should be sorry that you should be wanting in serving him on account of being

Misinformed of his real character; I should be afflicted if you were,

As some other gentlemen have been, misled on that score, who now esteem him,

And those among the best of my friends; wherefore, and from no other motive

I think it my duty to advertise you that you are most particularly desired,

To have especial attention to all he does, to show him all the respect imaginable,

Nor venture to say anything before him that may either offend or displease him

In any sort; for I may truly say there is no man I love so much as M. Compigne,

None whom I should more regret to see neglected, as no one can be more worthy to be

Received and trusted in decent society. Base, therefore, would it be to injure him.

And I well know that as soon as you are made sensible of his virtues, and

Shall become acquainted with him, you will love him as I do;
    and then
You will thank me for this my advice. The assurance I enter-
    tain of your
Courtesy obliges me to desist from urging this matter to you
    further, or
Saying anything more on this subject.

And now, the real message. By dividing the message in half in the proper places, Richelieu's honest appraisal of M. Compigne is revealed in the left column.

M. Compigne, a Savoyard by birth,
                      a Friar of the Order of Saint Benedict,
is the man who will present to you
                        as his passport to your protection.
this letter. He is one of the most
                        discreet, the wisest and the least
meddling persons that I have ever known
                        or have had the pleasure to converse with.
He has long earnestly solicited me
                        to write to you in his favor, and
To give him a suitable character,
                        together with a letter of credence;
Which I have accordingly granted to
                        his real merit, rather I must say, than to
His importunity; for, believe me, sir,
                        his modesty is only exceeded by his worth.
I should be sorry that you should be
                        wanting in serving him on account of being
Misinformed of his real character;
                        I should be afflicted if you were,
As some other gentlemen have been,
                        misled on that score, who now esteem him,
And those among the best of my friends;
                        wherefore, and from no other motive

I think it my duty to advertise you

                that you are most particularly desired,

To have especial attention to all he does,

                to show him all the respect imaginable,

Nor venture to say anything before him

                that may either offend or displease him

In any sort; for I may truly say there is

                no man I love so much as M. Compigne,

None whom I should more regret to see

                neglected, as no one can be worthy to be

Received and trusted in decent society.

                Base, therefore, would it be to injure him.

And I well know that as soon as you

                are made sensible of his virtues, and

Shall become acquainted with him,

                you will love him as I do; and then

You will thank me for this my advice.

                The assurance I entertain of your

Courtesy obliges me to desist from

                urging this matter to you further, or

Saying anything more on this subject.

TWO-FISTED GENIUS

The great Leonardo da Vinci is said to have been able to draw with his right hand while simultaneously writing with his left hand. More remarkable, the writing he did for the five thousand pages of his notebooks was often written backward, as a kind of personal code, perhaps to ward off eavesdroppers who would not understand or appreciate his far-reaching investigations of the human body, trees, plants, and stars. Such prudence was advisable in an age when research and intellectual freedom challenged the very order of society and risked the wrath of the Church.

In astronomical matters, the Church had declared that the sun, moon, and stars revolved around the earth, and brooked no dispute of that reality. Unintimidated, da Vinci studied the sun and stars and made exhaustive drawings and notes of planetary movement in his notebooks. One remarkable page contains a sentence that surely would have brought punishment, even jail, to da Vinci if it had been discovered. It certainly flew in the face of conventional wisdom in the 1490s. In code it read:

EVOM TON SEOD NUS EHT

25:

NEW MEDIA

ONE OF THE TENETS of game theory is that there are only a few basic gambits or tactics in any game devised by man. The pieces may change, the board may change, the mechanics of a game may change, the rules may be very complex, but underneath it all, experts say, there are but a handful of attack/bluff/feint/defend fundamentals to guide play in any game.

Codes offer a parallel truism. There are only a few basic strategies to communicate secretly, while the tactics or techniques within those basic strategies might number in the thousands. The secret message game is simply an evolving variation on a few basic themes.

Technology usually supplies all the new variations, and that is why computers play such a big part of modern code work. But every field of research—not just computers—holds intriguing possibilities for those who wish to hide secret messages.

THE MESSAGE IN THE MOLECULE

Dr. Carter Bancroft and other researchers at Mount Sinai School of Medicine may have pushed the technology frontier for code practice to a whole new level when, in 1999, they published their findings regarding a way to hide a secret message within human DNA. They further discussed a way to transfer the DNA to a small black dot that could sit, invisibly, on a printed period in an ordinary letter.

DNA science has reached the stage of sophistication in which manipulation and creation of DNA strands is daily laboratory practice. It occurred to Dr. Bancroft that, given the complexity of DNA—there are 30 million unique nucleotide strands in the molecule—it might be feasible to create messages from synthesized DNA strands and bury them so deep in the core of the DNA that no one but the intended recipient would know where to look for them.

To test their theory, they created a message and set about coding it into DNA. First they created a simple substitution code, assigning each letter of the alphabet to a three-nucleotide sequence called a triplet. (There are only four basic nucleotides—named A, C, G, and T—but they can be combined in millions of ways.) The key looked like this:

A = CGA	J = AGT	S = ACG
B = CCA	K = AAG	T = TTC
C = GTT	L = TGC	U = CTG
D = TTG	M = TCC	V = CCT
E = GGC	N = TCT	W = CCG
F = GGT	O = GGA	X = CTA
G = TTT	P = GTG	Y = AAA
H = CGC	Q = AAC	Z = CTT
I = ATG	R = TCA	

The numbers were: 1 = ACC, 2 = TAG, 3 = GCA, 4 = GAG, 5 = AGA, 6 = TTA, 7 = ACA, 8 = AGG, 9 = GCG.

Next, in the laboratory they created their message by sequencing the triplets as if they were letters in the alphabet, by using the substitution key. The messages were sixty-nine nucleotides long, and to them were added "marker" sequences on each end to act as flags for decoders who knew the markers and thus could find the "message" strands within the millions of possibilities. Then they placed the new strands randomly within the normal DNA bundle.

To transfer the message the DNA was applied via pipette to a printed black dot on filter paper, carefully cut into even tinier dots, glued over a period in a normal business letter, and mailed.

With those four basic steps they created a code sending/receiving system that has an incredibly high degree of integrity and security. To break the code, one would first have to find the "microdot" within the letter—a feat in itself. Having found it, one would have to recognize it as DNA, and have the resources to analyze it. Then, without knowing the marker sequence that identifies the target strand, one would be faced with looking at up to 30 million possible locations for the message. How would one do that? One couldn't, really—not without knowing the comprehensive sequence of all human DNA, and so far no one does. But let's say one defies probability and does find it. Then the decoder would have to identify the sequences that constitute the message, then use traditional code-breaking techniques to try to divine the substitution code and ultimately read the message.

This system, to current cryptanalysts, presents a series of blocks to decryption so formidable that it just may be unbreakable. It is a system so sophisticated that it employs advanced molecular biology as a starting point, and presents trial-and-error solution scenarios in such dizzyingly high numbers that any attempt to decrypt is discouraged from the beginning. However, for the holders of the two keys—the substitution code and the marker sequence—the system is quite easy and fast to use.

So what was the message hidden in the DNA? Here is what a sequence map of the strand looked like:

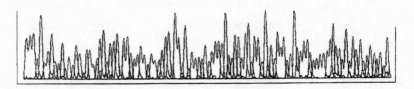

No clue? Here are the triplet keys the graph indicates:

AGT CTG TCT GGC TTA ATG TCT CCT CGA ACG ATG GGA TCT TCT GGA
TCA TCC CGA TCT TTG AAA

By referring to the substitution code above you'll get the answer—
"June 6 invasion Normandy"

INTERNET MESSAGES

The number of Americans participating in online group discussions in
chat rooms has grown exponentially in the last few years. As happened
with Morse Code a century earlier, chat roomers have developed a system of shortcuts and abbreviations to increase the delivery speed of
their communications. The system may have started as a secret language among chat room pals, but today it has gone mainstream.

Emoticons are symbols constructed of type characters and punctuation marks that denote emotions. They are meant to be viewed from
the side (so turn the symbols ninety degrees clockwise). Of the ap-
proximately 150 symbols in use, these are some of the most common:

:)	smiling
;)	winking
:D	grinning
:'(	crying
0:)	angel
:(	frowning
:/	frustrated
:*)	kiss
:0	surprised
:[	not talking
: p	tongue out

LOLs (see below) are acronyms, created for the same reason and in
the same spirit as the Morse acronyms of the late nineteenth century.

Some of the common ones you'll see in most chat room discussions are:

AFK = Away From Keyboard
BAK = Back At Keyboard
BRB = Be Right Back
BTW = By The Way
GMTA = Great Minds Think Alike
IMHO = In My Humble Opinion
LOL = Laugh Out Loud
OIC = Oh, I See
ROFL = Rolling On Floor, Laughing
TTFN = Ta-Ta For Now
WTG = Way To Go

WATSON! QWERTYUIO! SOS!

Although the message was not as dramatic as Alexander Graham Bell's "Watson, come here, I need you!" the moment was of similar import.

The year was 1971. The event was one of the many seemingly innocent milestones in the evolution of the computer. In this case, like Bell's, it had to do with communication. In 1958, the Department of Defense developed a system to link remote computers to each other so they could share massive files by virtue of computer links and language protocols. It was a bold plan presciently seeing a future when battles would be won by disabling a country's technology rather than its soldiers (as might happen during the electromagnetic pulse of a thermonuclear bomb). ARPANET, as it was called, came into being, and was the predecessor to today's Internet.

But it wasn't until 1971 that you could actually send messages over the net, ARPA or otherwise. In 1971 an unassuming computer engineer by the name of Ray Tomlinson put two computers side by side in his makeshift laboratory and tried to send a message from one to the other. After several false starts, he finally heard the bell and looked at the screen.

It said, "You Have a Message." E-mail was born.

But there's more to the story than that. Have you ever noticed the device between your name and the address? It looks like this: @. Ray Tomlinson also invented the use of the @ symbol as a means of identifying people and their discrete addresses. Why did he choose @? It was a matter of convenience. It was a single-digit character and it was already on the typewriter keyboard. That was that! Tomlinson, incidentally, didn't patent his idea. It was just a whim. He distributed copies of his e-mail program for free.

But what of his first message? Tomlinson isn't sure what he sent. He was just having fun, after all. Tinkering. He thinks it was QWERTYUIOP—the keys across the top of a typewriter keyboard—but it could have been TESTING. He just doesn't remember.

And, unfortunately, he was alone. There was no Watson on the other end.

THE ARECIBO INTERSTELLAR MESSAGE

Radio messages shoot into deep space travel at 186,000 miles per second, or the speed of light. By comparison, the *Voyager* spacecraft sails into the cosmos at a fraction of that speed. Even with its twenty-two-year head start, the *Voyager* spacecraft will be caught and passed in a few hours by tonight's Seinfeld rerun. That's why, on the occasion of the rededication of the radio telescope at Arecibo (Puerto Rico) in 1974, scientists wanted to use radio astronomy to send a message to the universe. The message was aimed at a cluster of stars called M13, some twenty-five thousand light-years from Earth. The odds of success, they figured, were much higher with a message traveling at cosmic speeds rather than Earth speeds. But, as with *Voyager* a few years later, what was it we wanted to say to the universe?

We wanted to explain ourselves, describe ourselves, let them know where we were and our level of technology, and we had to do it without benefit of the kind of solid objects that *Voyager* carried. The Arecibo message attempted to suggest the biological basics of human existence and do it with radio waves only. The message, therefore, is "written" in two radio frequencies, which, when arrayed in a pattern suggested by prime numbers, creates a two-dimensional picture. Here is the binary representation of what we sent to the stars on November 16, 1974, at 1:00 P.M. Atlantic Standard Time. Ten characters were transmitted per second by switching the Arecibo radio transmitter between two radio frequencies.

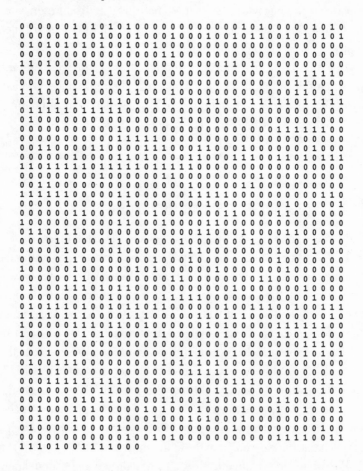

Ideally, the recipients of this message will use the following logic to decrypt the message. What they will deduce first is that the message contains 1,679 bits of information—that is, there are 1,679 ones and zeros in the transmission. Why that number and not, say, 1,700? In the process of figuring out why, they will soon recognize that 1,679 is the product of two prime numbers, 23 and 73 (numbers divisible only by themselves and one). That should lead them toward the idea that the message should be arranged in some combination of those two numbers. How about 73 rows of 23 numbers? Laid out that way, and converting the 0s to white squares and the 1s to black squares, the message yields no patterns or purposeful shapes. But turned the other way, in 23 columns of 73 numbers, a pattern appears! Anyone would recognize it as a deliberate expression and correctly assume it to be the message. Part of the grid yields two-dimensional pictograms; other parts are scientific notations and expressions.

Can you decipher the message? It really is extensively informative about us and our world.

The top pattern is the number progression 1 through 10, written in binary code, with 1 on the right, 10 on the left.

Below that is the number construction 1, 6, 7, 8, and 15. They are the atomic numbers of the essential elements of human life — (from right to left) hydrogen, carbon, nitrogen, oxygen, and phosphorus.

The next two rows of characters are binary representations of chemical formulas of the sugars and bases of human DNA.

The familiar double helix of the DNA molecule winds around a number representing the 4 billion nucleotide pairs existing in a single human chromosome, a number that could suggest our level of evolution and intelligence.

The bottom curve of the double helix envelops the head of the human body figure, suggesting the important relationship and connection between DNA and the manifest human form.

To the right of the human figure is an indication of its height, expressed as a factor of the only unit of measurement available — that of the wavelength on which the message was sent. That length was 2,380 Megahertz, or 12.6 centimeters. To the left of the figure is a number representing the population of the Earth. Below the figure is a diagram of our solar system, with nine planets and their proximity to the sun. Earth, the third planet, is diverted from the line of the other planets, denoting its location in the solar system, and suggesting it as the "home" of both the message and the human figure it almost touches.

Finally, the bottom arrangement is an illustration of the radio telescope that sent the message, with the diagonal lines suggesting the means of radio transmission. Below this is an indication of the diameter of the telescope, about one thousand feet, which would suggest our current level of technology.

So, astonishingly, our simple two-toned radio transmission packs quite an informational wallop. It indicates who we are; what we are made of; where we live; how big we are; how many of us there are; how smart we are; and how we are communicating. One can only imagine the impact it will have on some world, somewhere. Will they "write" us back? In fifty thousand years, we'll know.

THE MILTON BERLE CONUNDRUM

In a modest way, we earthlings have turned our radio-astronomic ear to the skies, listening for signs of life, and we have even had the temerity to send out a few hopeful messages. But scientists say that our deliberate messages probably won't be the ones our space neighbors will get. What will crash-land into their receivers will probably be a jumbled cacophony of radio and television shows, which started their cosmic journeys with the advent of broad-band radio and have reached their crescendo just now with the proliferation of global television transmissions. Imagine what a discordant mess our signals will be! Milton Berle and Ernie Kovacs, automobile commercials and football games, presidential debates and *Saturday Night Live*, film of World War II and Vietnam, *Dallas* and *Dynasty*, not to mention the programming from every other nation in the world, all arriving in a torrential stream-of-consciousness that to another civilization might be as murky and impenetrable as their own search for the meaning of life. But they will see patterns, and soon they will know that this is not random radio static. They will be compelled to solve our secret message. How will they start? Will they set about trying to establish frequency tables, just as our decoders would do here on Earth? If they can convert the energy to visual material, what will they make of *The Gong Show*? Or *The Godfather*? Or pornography?!

We can only speculate. But isn't it fascinating to consider that right now, out there in space, hurtling at the speed of light, is a wave front of radio energy emanating from Earth that contains a century of our planet's hopes and dreams, history and culture (high and low)? All of which may splash as if from a great height on another world, which will only listen as if to a secret message and wonder what it all means.

RESOURCES

Aaseng, Nathan. *Navajo Code Talkers.* New York: Walker, 1992.

Ambrose, Stephen E. *D-Day: The Climactic Battle of World War II.* New York: Simon & Schuster, 1995.

Arden, Harvey, and Steve Wall. *Wisdomkeepers: Meetings with Native American Spiritual Elders.* Hillsboro, Ore.: Beyond Words Pub Co., 1990.

Augarde, Tony. *The Oxford Guide to Word Games.* New Haven: Oxford University Press, 1984.

Brandreth, Gyles. *The Joy of Lex.* New York: William Morrow, 1980.

Campbell, Joseph. *The Power of Myth.* New York: Doubleday, 1988.

Corinda, D. *13 Steps to Mentalism.* New York: Robbins & Co., 1968.

Coy, Peter, "Online Auctions: Going . . . Going . . . Gone . . . Sucker!" *Business Week,* March 20, 2000.

Denton, Jeremiah, and Ed Brandt. *When Hell Was In Session.* Philadelphia: Smith-Morley, 1976.

Doyle, Sir Arthur Conan. *The Adventures of Sherlock Holmes.* New York: Buccaneer Books, 1986 library printing.

DuMont, E. R. *The Works of Voltaire.* New York: St. Hubert Guild, 1901.

Eiss, Harry Edwin. *Dictionary of Language Games, Puzzles and Amusements.* New York: Greenwood Press, 1986.

Fraser, Lady Antonia. *Mary, Queen of Scots.* New York: Delacorte Press, 1969.

Gresham, William Lindsay. *Houdini: The Man Who Walked Through Walls.* New York: Henry Holt, 1959.

Harper, Timothy. "e-mailman." *Sky Magazine,* October 1999.

Hattersley, Roy. *Nelson*. New York: Saturday Review Press, 1974.

Hay, Henry, ed. *Cyclopedia of Magic*. New York: Dover Publications, 1949.

———. *Hoffman's Modern Magic*. New York: Dover Publications, 1949.

Kahn, David. *Kahn on Codes: Secrets of the New Cryptology*. New York: Macmillan, 1983.

Kinder, Gary. *Ship of Gold in the Deep Blue Sea*. New York: Atlantic Monthly Press, 1998.

Larson, Erik. *Isaac's Storm*. New York: Crown Publishers, 1999.

Liungman, Carl G. *Thought Signs, The Semiotics of Symbols*. Santa Barbara, Calif.: IOS Press, 1995.

Marks, Leo. *Between Silk and Cyanide: A Codemaker's War*. New York: The Free Press, 1998.

Maurer, David W., with Luc Sante. *The Big Con*. New York: Anchor Books, 1999 reissue.

Mead, William B. *The Inside Game*. Alexandria, Va.: Redefinition, 1991.

Newsletter of the Astronomical Society of the Pacific, No. 20, Spring 1992, "The Search for Extraterrestrial Intelligence."

Olsen, Jack. *The Mad World of Bridge*. New York: Holt, Rinehart and Winston, 1960.

Packard, Vance. *The Hidden Persuaders*. New York: Pocket Books, 1984.

Randall, William Sterne. *Benedict Arnold: Patriot and Traitor*. New York: William Morrow, 1990.

Randi, James. *An Encyclopedia of Claims*. New York: St. Martin's Press, 1995.

Rhodes, Richard. *Dark Sun: The Making of the Hydrogen Bomb*. New York: Simon & Schuster, 1995.

Rochester and Kiley. *Honor Bound: The History of American Prisoners of War in Southeast Asia 1961–1973*. Washington, D.C.: Historical Office, Office of the Secretary of Defense, 1998.

Ryan, Cornelius. *The Longest Day*. New York: Simon & Schuster, 1956.

Sagan, Carl. *Cosmos*. New York: Random House, 1980.

———. *Murmurs of Earth*. New York: Random House, 1978.

Singh, Simon. *The Code Book: The Evolution of Secrecy From Mary, Queen of Scots to Quantum Cryptography*. New York: Doubleday, 1998.

Stoecklein, David R. *Cowboy Gear*. Ketchum, Idaho: Stoecklein, 1994.

Tobin, Jacqueline, and Raymond Dobard. *Hidden in Plain View: The Secret Story of Quilts and the Underground Railroad*. New York: Doubleday, 1998.

U.S. Air Force Yearbook. Bristol, England: The Royal Air Force Benevolent Fund Enterprises, 1999.

U.S. Department of Defense. *Nuclear Weapons Accidents, 1950–1980*. The Department of Defense, 1980.

U.S. Department of Energy. *Excerpts from Operation Hardtack*, a film. Las Vegas, Nev.: The Department of Energy, 1958.

U.S. Government Printing Office, "Know Your Money" and "New Designs for Your Money."

Wind, Herbert Warren, ed. *The Realm of Sport*. New York: Simon & Schuster, 1966.

FROM THE INTERNET

William A. Breniman's Internet posting of the last radio messages for the *Titanic*.

America Online: *How to LOL Online* (and with our thanks to the numerous people that explained this to us in the chat rooms).

Crowell, William P. *Introduction to the VERONA Project*. National Security Agency, 1997, NSA website.

Momsen, Bill. *Codebreaking and Secret Weapons of World War II*. Nautical Brass Magazine Online, 1996.

Soares, Eric. *Hand Signals for Sea Kayakers*. Bay Area Sea Kayaker's website, 1991 (and to our sea guides at Bar Harbor, Maine).

United States Secret Service website.

Crane and Hoist Hand Signals. Canadian Centre for Occupational Health & Safety. Posted on their website, 1999.

The D/FW Frequency List (and with our thanks to the police forces in Indian Hills, Kentucky, Los Angeles, California, and Austin, Texas).

Flight Deck Crew. Training Squadron Seven, Carrier Qualifications, USS *John F. Kennedy*, 1998. Posted on their website.

Hazardous Weather Policy. United States Naval Academy. Posted on their website: 2000.

Helicopter Hand Signals. Occupational Safety & Health Administration. Posted on their website: 1999.

Introduction to Hand Signals. Chicago Mercantile Exchange. Posted on their website: 2000 (and to our friends at PaineWebber for many examples).

Pavlof 1996 Eruption Summary. The Alaska Volcano Observatory. Posted on their website: 1999.

INDEX